My JOURNEY,
My LOS MAN

My JOURNEY, *My* LOS MAN

The Day I Started Paying Attention
to the Voice in My Head.
God Still Talks to His Children,
and I Am a True Witness.

DARNICE HARRISON

CITI OF
BOOKS

CITIOFBOOKS, INC.
3736 Eubank NE Suite A1
Albuquerque, NM 87111-3579
www.citiofbooks.com
Hotline: 1 (877) 389-2759
Fax: 1 (505) 930-7244

Ordering Information:

Quantity sales. Special discounts are available on quantity purchases by corporations, associations, and others. For details, contact the publisher at the address above.

Printed in the United States of America.

ISBN-13:   Softcover   979-8-89391-787-1
                    eBook   979-8-89391-788-8

Library of Congress Control Number: 2025913528

TABLE OF CONTENTS

Acknowledgements

First, I give all honor to God for allowing me to have such a beautiful testimony.

And second, I give a huge thank-you to everyone who shared this journey with me. I love you all.

Introduction

Through this season, I can only explain the way I feel as *wonderfully stunned*. I heard this song named "Gracefully Broken." It touched me to tears and made me realize that God is gracefully breaking me. And for that I am wonderfully shocked. I never knew that he loved me this much. But I always felt different from my family.

I mean I know that God loves me, but my guilt and shame kept me from listening to God. When I think of the things that I had done in my past, the guilt sometimes overwhelms me. Yet God wants me to get to know him and trust him wholeheartedly. I didn't realize that God still speaks to us right now in this day and age. I can't recall when I got lost, nor how it took me this long to realize that I am an angel of God—Earth Walker. Wow! God has been talking to me my entire life. I often thought that my thoughts and desires were mine as well as my talents.

During this season, on August 28, 2017, my youngest son, Carlos, was in a terrible car accident where he suffered some severe injuries and was in a coma. During my darkest days, I turn to God, and this time I had to listen because God wanted me to show my love to him as well.

My world felt so confusing, yet so wonderful. I had episodes of crying because of my sadness for Carlos and, then again, because of the wonderful feelings I have as I think of the goodness of the Lord, even while my heart is aching from the pain that I feel for my son. I mean he was only twenty-one, with the temper of a bull and a heart of gold.

I had learned that God will get your attention one way or the other. He will send people in your path to deliver his message. If God has chosen you, he will get you and give you chance after chance until he feels you are listening to him. In my lifetime, I can recall my name being called on two separate occasions by a man's voice.

I began to focus on ways to get to know God better. I pray daily. I make sure that God is first on my mind when I awake. I seek the Holy Spirit to assist me throughout my day. I read my Bible daily, and right now, I'm listening to the audio Bible so that I can hear it in its entirety. I journal again, listen to Joyce Meyer, Pastor Vernon, and a few more on YouTube and podcasts. It seems everything I hear and read has something to do with my life during this season. I'm not sure why God chose me, but he did, and for that I am grateful.

The Accident

"**S**omeone is chasing us," Carlos tells his friend as he races down highway I-480.

"No, they ain't," says the friend. "You just paranoid."

"No, I'm not. I remember his face."

And then silence.

The friend used Find My Location to locate Carlos and found a car accident. Carlos and the passenger were lying on the street feet apart. Someone had put flares around Carlos's limp body, and the passenger was on the other side of the barrier. The car he was driving had slammed into a parked car on the shoulder of the highway. Someone posted that they witnessed an accident on I-480 where two people were thrown from the car. Another witnessed two people stop to place flares around a body, and a report was called in to the police of two cars speeding down the highway. That was the last phone call and the last time anyone heard Carlos's voice.

On August 28, 2017, I received a phone call at 3:23 a.m. from my son Chaz, telling me that my youngest son was in a car accident, and from the looks of the car at the scene, it didn't look good. I got up and put some clothes on and headed for Metro Health Emergency. Chaz

1

and his girlfriend at the time were already there sitting in the waiting room of the ER. They both had scared blank looks on their faces. I asked Chaz what happened, and he told me that Carlos was speeding on I-480W at about one hundred miles per hour. My heart sank, and I grew numb. Why would he be driving that fast? He lost control of the car and hit a parked unoccupied vehicle that was on the exit ramp. In the car with Carlos was his female friend. Both were thrown from the vehicle upon impact. They both suffered head injuries, broken necks, and femurs. Her head injuries were more severe, and she also had more broken bones. They were both battling for their lives. We had a hard time getting in touch with the girl's family because she had no ID on her. After a few phone calls, the hospital reached her family.

When I got to the third-floor trauma unit where Carlos was taken, the waiting room was filled with the girl's family members. I didn't recognize any of them. A woman came through the trauma floor doors and said that her grandma was back there to give an identification of the girl. My heart sank. All I could think was *Is it that bad?* She said that she didn't even look like herself. That really gave me chills even though I had never seen her before. We didn't know if either of them would make it. She was scheduled to have her brain surgery first so that they could release some of the fluid from her brain. When they took a look at her again, they said that her body was in too much shock, and she wouldn't be able to handle it. The injuries were too severe.

Oh, God was all I could think. I was watching her family and friends as they were in disbelief, panicking and crying. Her aunt said if she made it through this, there is a God.

I replied, "There is a God. She will make it. She will make it." I started praying silently and rapidly. Her grandma came out, and I hugged her as she hugged me. I told her that I was so, so sorry over and over again as we both cried and rocked. I had been sitting on the other side of the room, not knowing what to do or say to her family. I kept trying to make myself get up. I attempted once and sat back down. I was so nervous and confused.

I was shown who her mother was, and when she sat down to cry, I sat on the arm of the chair and put my arm across her shoulders to give her a hug and told her that I was so, so sorry as well. She looked up at me and walked away. That was what I was afraid of happening, my heart sank. I don't believe she knew who I was at the time. We all gathered around the waiting room, held hands as a woman that was an ordained minister led us in prayer. After the prayer, we heard loud cries, and the family was told to go say goodbye to her because she wasn't going to make it.

My family and I were allowed to go back and see Carlos. Oh my god, he looked so beat up. His head was swollen almost twice its size. He had on a neck brace, scars, and blood all over his face. I just felt numb, in disbelief of all that was happening.

I went to his bedside and said, "Oh, Los, you really messed yourself up this time." I just held his hand and examined every scar on his body. His elbow was bandaged, lip busted, gash on the right side of his head. He just looked awful. I felt so sorry for him. I prayed over him and noticed that her room was next door. Her aunt came to me and asked me if I wanted to say goodbye to her. I was feeling so guilty for praying for my child to live while she was dying, and my son was the driver of the accident. I mean, are you supposed to do that? I felt bad for the children, the families, and myself. Lord, I was so confused at all that was going on; I hadn't even come to the realization of it all.

I hesitated as she put her arm around my waist and asked me again. She spoke so lovingly and softly. She told me that it was okay as she waited on my response. I was so nervous. I nodded as she repeated and held my waist tight. So I let her lead me into the room where she was.

Carlos's room number was 133, and at this moment, I can't recall her room number.

Oh, how my eyes filled with tears, and my heart pounded. I was so scared to see her. As I approached her room, I could see her head. I trembled with the thought of the pain she must've been in. She had a neck brace on and a tube in her nose and mouth. I slowly walked into the room and stood by her bedside. I told her that I was sorry this had happened to her as I touched her hand. It looked like her entire body was swollen. I prayed over her. Her family was scattered throughout the hallway, and a few were in the room.

The family and I gathered around her bedside, held hands, and said a prayer as we watched the numbers on the monitor fall. Her mom laid her head on her baby's belly and said "Please don't leave me." This was a very sad moment. I hugged the young lady on my right side and rubbed the young lady's back on my left. I was feeling so terrible about her situation, and my heart was pouring out for her family's pain. At the same time, my heart was aching for my own child's recovery and life. Never had my heart ached with such pain for someone else as it ached for myself simultaneously. The pain was so unreal. Her aunt came over to Carlos's room and asked how he was doing and if she could go in and see him as well as another one of the relatives. They both wished him a good recovery.

As we were sitting outside of Carlos's room, her mom walked by crying, and yet as her daughter lay in her bed deceased, she said that she felt sorry for Carlos as well. Carlos's Dad and I thanked her and apologized again. I believe I stumbled over my words and said, "I just don't know what to say." I had my mom, sisters-in-laws, uncles, brother, and his dad there until the late hours of the night. I was speechless and so in shock. I got a wet towel and began to wipe the dried blood from his face. My uncle didn't think it was a good idea, but I told him I didn't want him looking like that. I couldn't tell what's going on, and the nurses weren't trying to wash it off, so I gently wiped as much dirt and blood from his face as I could.

After about an hour or so, I was told that he had injuries to his head and needed a bolt put in his head to measure and keep track of the swelling on his brain. Of course, I agreed to have it done. When they finished with the procedure, Carlos had a thick roll of gauge sticking up from his forehead with a tube coming out. This scared me. I wasn't prepared for how it would look.

I said, "Damn, I didn't know that he was going to look like a unicorn."

His dad chuckled, but I was serious at that moment, because that was the first thing that came to mind when I had seen him. Man, oh man, did my heart ache. I prayed for God to send his angels down to help my son recover. All I could do was stare at Carlos and cry. Seeing him like that was tearing my soul apart. My nerves were going wild. I couldn't stop thinking about her loss of life and how her mom must be feeling, to lose her only daughter. I have one daughter, and I know that would've damn near destroyed me.

The nurses and doctors were very kind to my family and myself. We stayed at the hospital long after visiting hours. Soon after, my family began to leave, and I started to feel lonely and even more helpless in this situation.

I stood next to Carlos's bedside and said again, "You really messed yourself up this time." I prayed over him and let him know that I loved him, and I needed him to pull through this. More tears as I tried to be strong. It was so hard to leave him there, but his dad stayed the night with him, and I went home.

August 29, 2017

I had a sleepless night, but I returned to the hospital bright and early. The doctor told us that he was going to need a brace on his leg to stabilize it for surgery. Again I didn't expect to see what I had seen as the finished result. They put a steel bar through his knee and had a bar hanging from it which had a weight on the end of it that hung over the bed. It looked very painful. He had a bandage on his elbow, and it had bled through it. He was still unconscious, and he had a contusion on his lungs which was another reason why he was on a ventilator. It causes difficulty in breathing. He had good reflexes, but it was too soon to tell what his injuries to his head were. The bolt in his head showed no changes so far.

I had to go to work today, but I wanted to spend a couple of hours with Los. I thought that I could go to work and be fine, but my co-workers could tell that something was wrong. When asked, I told them my son was in a car accident last night and told them of his condition. They were shocked and asked why I was there. I said because there's nothing that I could do for him, and I needed to keep busy. And bills still have to be paid. A few tears fell and, I pulled myself together.

Well, within five minutes, another coworker hugged me and said she was sorry. Immediately, my eyes filled up with tears and said, "This is why I don't do hugs." I walked to the back and just cried. After I got myself together, I went back out to the restaurant and tried again. Nope, it was done now, crying spells. I stayed at work for about forty minutes and had to leave.

Today is my mom's birthday, and she said it's all about Carlos right now.

August 30, 2017

Carlos had a rough night. He had fever since the twenty-eighth. They couldn't seem to get it under control. They had him on pain meds, Fentanyl and Tylenol. He coughed and had to have his mouth suctioned from the phlegm. He was still unconscious. I tried not to get too hopeful when I saw him move because the doctor said it was just spontaneous movement due to the brain trying to repair itself.

My sister-in-law swore that he was moving on command for them. I didn't blow their joy. I just nodded my head. I tried to see things for the way they are. I was hopeful and prayerful. I prayed with my Los Man daily as well as for him. I also thanked God for each day that I have with him. My mind tried not to think of the worst and be strong. My heart ached like there was a knot in it that wouldn't loosen. I had support around me, and the doctors and nurses were kind for the most part.

My daughter would have a surprise proposal on September 3, 2017. I was supposed to leave for Vegas to be with her on September 2, 2017. This was planned a month ago. I was so torn as to whether I should go or not. I didn't want to leave Los, but I knew she needed me, and I needed her as well. Still no progress from Los. He was stable right now. The doctors were discussing whether to remove the bolt out of his head since there had been no swelling.

I was so numb, and my heart ached constantly. My mind was always on Los's future and progress. I couldn't talk about him to anyone without crying. The words would not come out. My aunt called me from out of state, and I couldn't speak. She understood. He is such a loving person, and when he would awake and realize that his friend didn't survive, oh, Lord, he is going to be devastated. I wanted him to remember so that he could tell me what happened. But at the same time, I didn't want him to remember because of what all came with the remembrance. That really made me sad knowing how sad he would be. He had gotten accepted to play basketball for CSU and had been practicing and was really looking forward to it.

Carlos had a long slow road of recovery ahead of him, and I would be there every step of the way when he woke up. I was staying the night with him, and my sister-in-law would be here in the morning to relieve me. She had been here every day and was such a blessing right now when his dad and I were not here. She's liked my head nurse. She asked all the questions that I wanted to ask. I appreciate her so much for helping us out. I stayed overnight most nights because his dad really couldn't afford to miss work, and I work flexible hours, so I could leave in the morning and go home to prepare for work. I only live five minutes from the hospital.

August 31, 2017

Today is my granddaughter's fourth birthday. Her grandmother on her mom's side sent me a picture of her and said that she hoped it made me smile. "It did," I replied.

Carlos's bolt had been removed, and I noticed that the bandage on his elbow had been bleeding for two days now. So I watched the nurse change the bandage so that I could see the scar. As I looked at it, I cringed. The nurse did as well, and she appeared shocked.

I said, "That's not a scar. That's a gash. Shouldn't it have three to four stitches?" She said, "Yeah, this is not a scar like I was told." She said that she would look into it. She changed the bandages and took notes for the orthopedic doctor.

Well, after the doctor checked his wound, they cleaned it and found gravel inside as well as a severed tendon. He was injected with a fluid to prevent infection and given antibiotics. He was scheduled for surgery on his elbow Tuesday.

I was still undecided about Vegas. The Lord knew I didn't want anything to happen to him while I was gone. My sister-in-law said I should go. Sher and his dad will look after him because Ciauna needed me. Carlos was still having fevers that spiked up and down. He would be getting an MRI soon to check for what was going on in his brain. He had an EEG hooked up to his brain and had to be on it for twenty-four hours to track the electrodes and activity in his brain. I was trying to keep abreast of everything involving my Los Man.

The day he went down to get his wound cleaned, my sister-in-law was supposed to call me when he finished. I was at work, awaiting word from her. My nerves were all mixed up because what was to be an hour ended up being 3–4 hours. So I left work to go check on Los. My sister-in-law texted me and apologized. She had fallen asleep. He had been back in less than an hour. Her sister was there by then and had told her. That was a relief.

I had been praying for peace, strength, and understanding for the girl's family. The worry of how her family felt about Carlos and I weighed heavy on my heart. I was aching for my son and her family. I prayed to God that they didn't want some sort of revenge and that they would forgive us. Although I had never met them, my heart ached just the same. I was confused of how I should feel. Is it wrong to want recovery for my child while another has lost their life in the accident where he was the driver?

As I was sitting in the waiting room with some of my family members, I was praying to God for the girl's family's forgiveness. I was just quietly awaiting a chance to go back and visit Los when my phone rang around 11:23 p.m. It was her mom with a soft sincere voice, I could tell that she had been crying. She had gotten my number from her sister. I had given it to her and told her if she needed anything from me to let me know. Somehow I had lost her number though.

Well, her mom told me that she just wanted to let me know that she didn't hate me, nor Carlos. Neither she nor her family was angry at us. They weren't holding any grudges, and she loves me. She also asked about Carlos. She said that they had a balloon send-off at CSU for her daughter, and she had the school announce that no one was to hold a grudge, nor treat Carlos any different. My heart immediately began to feel a sense of relief as tears rolled down my face. I whispered, "Thank you, Lord."

I told her how much I appreciated her calling. "And again, I'm so sorry for your loss."

By the end of the conversation, she was in tears. She also stated that she talked to her family, and they are not bad people. She invited me and my family to the funeral and the events for the weekend.

That was one of many prayers that God had answered for me, and it lifted a heavy weight off my heart. I had ordered flowers to be sent to the funeral home for the girl the day before and was wondering how her mom and family were going to feel about it. I had seen on Facebook that she liked the color purple and was asking for everyone to wear purple to her funeral. So I sent purple and lavender flowers with a purple bow and a card that read "With our deepest sympathy, Darnice Harrison and family."

I'm glad to know that she accepted the flowers.

I was hesitant about attending the funeral, so his dad and I said that we would go view the body. I didn't feel strong enough to go to the funeral, didn't want the whispers and stares. I'm just a little shy around strangers and felt it was too soon for the family. Well, I didn't make it to the viewing; it just hurt too bad.

September 1, 2017

I had decided to go and be with Ciauna. She was very upset, and I could feel her pain seeing as she was so far away. We FaceTimed each other, and she spoke to Carlos. She was not quite ready to see him, so I put the phone to his ear so that she could talk to him. My mind was still baffled about leaving Carlos, yet I knew my daughter needed a mother's hug. My younger sister took a last-minute flight to Vegas to see her, and that made her smile. I was thankful for that. She is so sweet. My son and I were supposed to surprise her on Sunday, but due to the circumstances, we thought it best to let her know we were there as soon as we got there. He arrived before me. She still didn't know about her surprise proposal. We needed a beautiful moment amid this sadness.

Due to it being Labor Day weekend, the MRI was postponed for a few days. There were not enough doctors on staff. Carlos made it through the night. He had coughing spells and hadn't had a bowel movement, so they'd been giving him meds to help. He was checked on every hour and turned every two hours. He showed minimal reaction to pain, didn't follow any commands such as blink, open eyes, or move toes. Nothing! This was so painful seeing my twenty-one-year-old, strong, athletic child lying here helpless. I whispered in his ear to please pull through. "Who's going to text me just to say I love you? You have to play basketball for CSU." I had frequent crying spells and quiet moments where I just stare into nothingness and think.

I never ever thought in a million years that I would be going through anything like this. My heart ached every moment of the day. I made it to work today, and one of my regular customers asked me how I was today. Actually, my answer for the day was "I'm living" or "Just okay." I was not sure what I said. I left work as early as I could so that I could get back to my Los Man. He still hadn't awoken yet.

September 2, 2017

Carlos made it through another night. God and his angels were still with him. I thank God for that. Today I was supposed to leave for Vegas. I was still hesitant to leave Carlos. His dad said go. One of my sisters-in-law said she wouldn't go. But I thought my daughter and I needed each other right now. All the while I was at work, I was worried about leaving my Los Man, praying that I didn't miss any progress or mishaps. My sister-in-law and his dad assured me that they would keep me updated. I was so anxious at work, and my nerves were rattled.

Ciauna had FaceTimed and texted me several times while en route to the airport. I kept cutting her short because I didn't want her to ask where I was at or going. I didn't want to lie to her or spoil my surprise visit. Once I arrived in Las Vegas, I had my son pick me up from the airport. I called my daughter's friend to tell him that I wanted to surprise her today. We got to the hotel, and I went into the room after my son. And my daughter just looked at me up and down with a look of confusion like she didn't know who I was. I was standing there wondering, *Well, do I get a hello?* I was confused at the moment at her reaction. She then brightened her eyes, opened her mouth with a shocked expression, and started to shake. She grabbed me around my waist and hugged me tight as she sobbed. I comforted her and rocked her for 5–7 minutes. She said it wasn't registering who I was. This was the best surprise ever.

We tried our best to enjoy this moment of joy for the weekend, and every silent moment we had, her friends would say something funny to try and keep our minds occupied. I was glad that I made the trip to be with her. A mother knows her child, and I knew she needed me. Our weekend was like a ray of sun shining through a cloudy day. I worried all weekend and had to stop myself from calling to check on Los at times. I did good, only called two times per day, and we texted in between. I returned home on September 4, 2017, at 4:30 a.m. Yes, my Los Man made it through the weekend. Thank you, Lord.

I know not to question God, for it is his will and his battle, but I find myself wanting to ask. Yet I didn't. I talked to myself and prayed when worry struck. Sometimes I would post my feelings and thoughts on Facebook, and I got a lot of kind words and encouragement. I would never lose hope, nor faith in this situation, for my God that I serve is good. And though I might not see the light now, I knew I would eventually. I just continued to pray for Los's recovery and strength, and I prayed for my own understanding and strength as well. I knew God would see me through, and He has Los's best at hand. I would pray and not worry. At least, I would give the worry part my best shot.

The Decision

September 6, 2017

I spent the night with Carlos, and he had been coughing up a lot of phlegm. His fever was down, but now he was sweating quite a bit. I enjoyed rubbing his feet and hands, in hopes that he felt my touch as I talked to him. I had clipped his toenails for him also. I wondered what he was thinking. He had never liked being away from home, not even for sleepovers at his grandparents' house, and they lived next door. I stayed with him until he fell asleep so that he wouldn't feel alone.

Today, in the morning, I received some bad news from the neurologist. He told me that the MRI read that his brain stem and the left and the right sides of his brain are severely damaged. This affected his motor skills, and he should be aware enough of the tube down his throat that he should be trying to pull it out. Also if pinched, he should grab your hand to stop you. For a second I thought, *Pinch? Why would you pinch him?* But he hadn't regained consciousness after three days of being off pain medicine.

The doctor said that we needed to have a family meeting and discuss further options with all doctors involved so that they could come up with the best solution and care for Carlos's quality of life. As he spoke to me, my legs began to shake. I was balling and twirling my hands together while my eyes filled with the tears that I was trying to fight back.

The doctor asked me if I had any questions. My mind was numb, and I was speechless. I asked if the brain stem could repair itself, and he said that he highly doubted it. My heart knotted up, and I cried uncontrollably. Thank God my sister-in-law Rita was there. She just held me and tried to soothe me. I called my mom and Chaz to tell them the news. Rita called her sisters. My family came to be by my side. We set the meeting for 2:00 p.m. the following day.

My heart ached like never before. Carlos had a couple of bowel movements, so the nurse decided to insert a tube in his rectum so that his bottom wouldn't get raw. There was this nurse named Clair. She was the most passionate of all the nurses that I had met there at the hospital. She sat down and asked me how I was doing. She listened to me on several occasions throughout the night. She's very sweet.

At one point during the wee hours of the night, I guess around 4:00 a.m., a male nurse came to assist Nurse Clair and said, "Isn't this patient already gone?" As I lay in the chair half asleep, my eyes opened. My heart sank, and I froze.

Nurse Clair replied, "No, no, no, he's fine." I never turned my head to let them know that I heard them.

I just lay there staring out the window while tears rolled down my face. After they left the room, I sat up and broke down with my face in my hands. It took me maybe an hour to recover from that. Also through the night, I heard Nurse Clair tell another nurse that Carlos opened his eyes three times. I believe that's what she said. The doctor made his rounds and confirmed what I had heard. I asked if that was good. He said yes, but we still had to take other measures (sigh). One good thing leads to one more hope.

September 7, 2017

I went home to freshen up, and the decision weighed heavy on my mind and heart. The doctor had asked me to decide whether to go full speed ahead with providing the best care for Carlos, or should we consider making him comfortable. I couldn't bear the thought of letting him go. He was so young, only twenty-one years old, headed for college to play basketball, and now he was lying in a hospital bed fighting for his life. This all seemed so unreal, like I felt as if God wouldn't have done something like this to me. I talk to him all the time, and I pray not regularly as I should, but I do. I know to confide in him, and he has always been there for me in times of trouble. So where is he now? I wanted to speak those words to God, but I couldn't bring myself to say it.

I sat on my couch and asked God what should I do. I asked because I didn't feel as if it was my decision to take a life, if that was going to be the case. I asked again as the doctor's words rang through my head, *Full speed ahead.* In one moment of silence, as I was about to ask God again what I should do, I heard a voice in my head say, *Full speed ahead.* I sat up and tilted my head to listen again as I asked again, and it repeated, *Full speed ahead.* I sat up straight with a knowing in my heart that it was not my voice, and there was a confidence in me.

I stood up and said, "Well, full speed ahead it is."

I got up and left to go to the hospital. Carlos made it through the night, and I was nervous about the meeting. I kept repeating to myself, *Full speed ahead.* Two-thirty seemed so far away. Soon my family would start coming in. His dad was running late because he went to work, and it was rush hour now. My brother and sister-in-law Debbie were the first ones there. I was just quiet and nervous, praying nothing had changed with Carlos. I felt as if it was all up to me, even though I knew it was up to God.

Well, my verse for today was to listen to the whispers of God and follow your heart. We were sent to wait in a family area and were given drinks and snacks as we waited for the doctors to come in. It felt as if all eyes were on me. His dad hadn't arrived, and the doctors had come to discuss what we wanted to do. I listened to them explain what was going on with Los, and some family members asked a few questions. The doctors said if he survived, he would need lots of care, and it would be a long slow road for him. He might never wake up, or he might. They couldn't say for sure. People have lived with the injuries that Carlos had for up to two years or more. It would take a miracle for him to ever fully recover.

When asked what I wanted to do, I said, "Well, God told me full speed ahead." The doctors said, "So you want us to do all we can for him to live?" And I said, "Yes, full speed ahead." I could see and feel the relief in the room after I spoke. The doctors said he could try palliative care, and he would go to a long-term-care facility. He would need lots of support, love, and care from his family and friends.

My family and I said, "Well, we are here to ride this journey for as long as it takes. This is a road with no right or left turns, so straight ahead we go." I told the doctors that we wanted to go full speed ahead to the next step available. Yes, I listened to God and my heart. So the journey began.

His dad came rushing in, asking what was going on, and he was told that I decided to do all we could to prolong his life. He was glad of the decision, and I wouldn't have made any other decision without him anyway. Carlos had a lot of secretions in his lungs, so he coughed a lot and had to be suctioned often. He looked as if the coughing hurts, and he had to strain. His air had been cut down to 30 percent, and he was doing good with breathing on his own. They had been taking him off the ventilator periodically to see how he handled breathing without it. Thank God. I stayed the night with him. I just couldn't leave him there alone just yet. So this was my life—work, home to change, and back to his bedside.

I rubbed his feet and hands to keep them soft as well as to provide him some touch and stimulation. My sister-in-law thought it was strange that I did this and even told me to leave his feet alone because she didn't like anyone touching her feet. Well, he's my child, and I planned to get a reaction from him as a result of this.

The Healing Begins

September 8, 2017

C arlos made it through the night. He was still full of secretions and coughed a bit, but he was still here. We thanked God each and every day for another moment, second, minute, and hour that we had to spend together. I prayed each night and played encouraging music with him.

Today, his dad, my brother, and I were visiting with Los, and Nurse Clair received a phone call. The caller asked if this was Carlos Harrison's room. I looked with surprise because I didn't know who was on the phone. The caller said, "This is the friend's family. We were checking on his status." I was shaking my head no, so the nurse told her that she couldn't release that info.

The caller said, "Okay, let the family know that we are concerned and hope he gets better."

Well, I thought I recognized the voice as the girl's aunt. So later I called her, but I didn't let her know that I heard the phone call earlier. She seemed to be very sincere about Carlos's status. I gave her an update and told her that he was still in a coma and fighting. She wished him a full recovery and told me that she loves us. I thanked her and hung up the phone with a sigh of relief.

I then called his dad back to let him know that I had talked to her, and he felt as if she was sincere about her concern. I still felt a little weird about her calling the hospital, but I dismissed the feeling. His dad was spending the night with him tonight.

September 9, 2017

Well, Los made it through the night, so God was still working. I had to work both jobs today, so I planned to go see Los before noon. I woke up around 9:30 or 10:00 a.m., and I was too sleepy. My body felt weak. Well, not weak, just tired, so I lay back down and woke up too late to go see Los before work. My day at work was going fine. I was waiting on his dad to send me a text with an update, but nothing. The closer it got to my time to leave work, the more my mind worried about how Los's day went. I thought of him constantly when I was away from him.

After I left my first job, I was missing Los, and I didn't have time to go see him before I went to my second job. I got a chance to talk to his dad, and he said that Carlos slept well and convinced me to go to work because he would be there. It was hard to rely on others for info. My heart ached, and I was just so worried that he might leave me while I was away. His dad didn't answer his text, nor called as frequently as I liked, and that left me to worry about Carlos's status, but I went to work anyway. Lord, help me, please.

Well, actually now that I think about it, Carlos didn't have a good night. His blood pressure spiked, and it took two different medications to get it under control. This was my first day back to my second job since the accident, and for some reason, I felt as if everything was new to me, maybe because I hadn't spoken to anyone about his status. This was why I didn't want to be at my job. My nerves were rattled, and I really wanted to be with Carlos.

I got to work about 4:10 p.m. or so, feeling nervous about people asking me about Los. When I got to the Skyline room where I would be working, I heard my name being called so happily as my manager told me he liked my hair. I get a few more hellos, but I was feeling so far away.

Then I heard the banquet coordinator call my name in a surprised yet joyful tone. "Darnice, hey, how's your son?" I tried to answer. I think I said he's in a coma. At the same time, I was thinking, *It's not a joyful experience I'm going through, and why are you so happy to ask me about it?* I left the room because I felt myself about to cry. I pulled myself together, went back into the room, and I just couldn't get my mind on the job. I felt lost.

I told my coworker that I was going to get glasses and start the waters for the tables. I grabbed a cart and started down the hallway. I heard my supervisor behind me asking me if I was okay. My eyes were already filled with tears, and I kept walking while replying no. He caught up with me and asked again if I was okay. I turned the corner and just melted, and I slid down the wall, sobbing and holding my face with my hands. I was trying to explain Carlos's status to him.

He said, "You can go home. I'll figure this out and talk to our manager." He's like, "Really, it's okay. You can go." I was a mess, so after about 3–4 minutes, I got myself together enough to move, and I went to my car and just sobbed some more for about another 3–4 minutes. I saw our manager had come out and sat on the dock to smoke. I could feel him looking at me but with sincerity.

I managed to pull off, and off to the hospital to be with Los I went. I walked into Los's hospital room, and his dad and my mom were there. I still felt numb as I spoke to them. They looked at me as if they were discussing me and didn't say anything. They both knew I was having a bad day. I was relieved to be with Carlos, and it took a few minutes for me to settle down.

His dad said that Carlos had been doing good, and he was just resting. He said that Los's nutrition was stopped because he vomited three times. James, his nurse, chimed in, "Yes, he's been really off since you left. Maybe it's that momma's chemistry he needs. He's been keeping me busy." I laughed a little and said, "Yes, maybe."

James is a very nice and caring nurse. We talked about him being in the military, and he told me how he had lost many friends and family. He said that he knew how I felt and told me from one parent to another, "Only you know what you should do and how you feel about Carlos. If you have any little light of hope, hold on to it because you are momma bear, and you will know when it's time to make a change. These doctors don't know everything. They go by science and measures. I've seen people come out of worse." As I was crying, I told him thank you because I believed Carlos was trying to come out. He responded to my sisters and others with his toes. James didn't seem too convinced in my eyes, but he still told me to hold on to all hope. So I would.

Positive Vibes

Just a few notes from looking back

September 4, here's a text from my sister-in-law:

> *Carlos is responding when me and Deb tells him to move his toes and blink his eyes!!!*

When I received this text, I didn't feel confident because the doctor told me that he was having simultaneous movements. But I didn't ruin her joy by telling her that.

Facebook posts and updates:

August 28:

> OMG, this is a tough one to deal with, please keep the other family and mine in your prayers today. We need prayer ever so badly.

> Hello, here's an update on my son Carlos Harrison. He's had surgery on his femur this morning and is currently undergoing surgery on his neck. It's so hard to see your once strong son helpless, yet even harder to lose one. Again, I'm

23

so sorry for the loss of life, and my prayers for strength and understanding goes out to her family.

August 29:

Hello, Facebook. I just want to say, as much as my heart aches for my son's recovery, it aches just as much for the other families' loss of life and her mom. I didn't raise a selfish young man. He is one of the most caring of all my sons. He would never purposely hurt anyone. Although on 8/28/2017, the decision he made was not a good one, yet he is still a young soul, and we all make decisions that we would like to take back. I know Carlos Harrison better than anyone in our family, and his dad and I can confess that we have never had a problem with him telling us the truth, no matter what the consequences were. So all I'm asking is that everyone please allow him time to heal and time to explain what happened on 8/28/2017. There are more people affected by his decision than him. We are not mean, evil-spirited people. I care, he cares, and God cares. We may not understand God's hand at times, but we do have to play the hand that we are dealt. This is one hand that's going to change Carlos's life forever, and I will be there every step of the way. To the other family, my heart will be with you all, and I will forever be here to assist in any way I can. Please don't hesitate to reach out to me for I will be reaching out to you. So as I write this statement, my eyes fill with tears, and my heart aches with sorrow, remorse, and confusion. This isn't easy for either family, though I know God will see us through, and there is a purpose for it although we may not see it, nor understand it. I still have faith that it will get better. Please continue to pray for strength for Carlos and the other family. We have a rocky road ahead of us. Thank you all for your time, prayers, kind words. Have a blessed day.

Darnice Harrison

Post from my cousin Jay:

I want to praise and thank the Lord in advance for Carlos healing. I pray for the family of the young lady that lost her life. Give them strength and understanding to know you make no mistakes. Lord, I pray that you receive the VICTORY out of all of this. I ask this in Jesus name. Amen

#HISBLOODSTILLWORKS

August 30:

Hello, everyone. Update for my son Carlos Harrison. Well, he made it through the night, and he is in stable condition. Please continue to keep him in your prayers, and thank you so much.

August 31:

Good morning, update for Carlos Harrison. He made it through the night and is still stable. Thank you all for your prayers and have a blessed day.

September 1:

Good evening FB, update for Carlos Harrison. My son is still stable. One day at a time. Sorry for the late update. Thank you for your prayers. Have a good night.

September 2:

Good morning FB. My Los Man had a rough night, but he made it. Thanks for your prayers and have a blessed day.

Lord, I don't know if I can ride this roller coaster. It's a rough one.

September 4:

Hello FB, Carlos Harrison made it through the night. One day at a time.

September 6:

Hey FB, update for my son Carlos Harrison. Well, it's a very gloomy day, please pray. Thank you.

September 7:

Feeling nervous. I just feel so numb, yet hopeful.

September 8:

Hey FB, update for my son Carlos Harrison. He had an uncomfortable day with coughing but restful night. Have a blessed day all.

September 9:

Hi FB, Carlos Harrison had a tough night. Please continue to pray. Thank you.

On September 10, I posted a picture of a cross and poem that I drew for Carlos. It's the first of a series of drawings of inspiration for him.

He Is Fighting

September 10, 2017

Carlos made it through the night, thank God. I was leaving the hospital to go home and get ready for work. I ran into my sister-in-law and her son. We talked for maybe 5–6 minutes before I took off. Later that day, I received a text from my sister-in-law saying that while she and my other sister-in-law and son were there, they were talking to Carlos, and he was moving his toes, and he yawned. "I knew he heard us." This made me smile, and I had a very confident day at work.

September 11, 2017

Carlos slept well and might be able to go to a regular floor today. Well, Carlos didn't go to a regular floor. His nutrition wouldn't stay down, and he hadn't had a bowel movement, so his nutrition was stopped, and he was given something to help move his bowels. But it didn't seem to be working, so I would wait until a little later on today. He was resting well, wasn't coughing as much during the day. Maybe he would get moved to a regular floor tomorrow.

I was spending the night with Los, and I would be off tomorrow so I could sleep in with him. Tonight he was coughing like every hour or so and sometimes hard. His eyes seemed to stay open longer after he coughed. I knew he was coming around, and God was working. I didn't talk to him much today because he seemed like he was enjoying the rest after not sleeping too well with all the coughing and suctioning every hour. At around 10:00 p.m., we said our prayers and thanked God for another day.

September 12, 2017

> The doctor started his nutrition at 20%, but after about 3 hours, they had to stop it, and the staples from his leg were removed. Right now he is resting.

This was a text from my sister-in-law. She was the best support right now. She took the best notes and asked the best questions. She had been here at the hospital every day since day one. Carlos was showing signs of awareness more when he got his throat suctioned, coughed, or got turned. He opened his eyes when these happened. It told me that he was aware that something was going on; he just couldn't say.

Last night, Carlos got a haircut by Nurse Clair. She did her best. It was a little patchy because she discovered some nicks along the way, but he looked better, and his hair smelled a lot better. Well, he was bald, but it would grow back. He looked like my Los Man now. While he was getting his haircut, his toes and feet were very active. I admit that I was a bit nervous because I couldn't tell whether that meant it hurt or not. I said to the nurse, "He knows what's going on, or he knows something is happening." She said, "He definitely knows something is going on." I felt even more confident about his progress. I videoed his reactions to getting a haircut and sent it to some family members. I believe they were just as excited. Thank you, Lord!

Carlos was still having trouble passing his bowels, and Nurse James had been working with him for the past few days to help him. He explained each step he took to help his bowels move, and he was trying not to have to try anything too severe.

September 13, 2017

My Los Man made it through the night. Thank God. He still hadn't let go of that stinky food, haha. I gotta add some form of humor for myself. I talked to Los as I rubbed his feet and hands. I told him that I knew he was fighting hard, but I needed him to concentrate and try working on the part of his brain that controls his bowels, because he really needed to drop that stinky load so that he could feel better and progress to the next level. I also asked God to put his healing hand on him and help him move in that area.

Still no poop, so Nurse James tried one more thing before trying a more aggressive strategy. He inserted a tube and gave Los some medicine through his IV to help him pass his bowels and to keep him from vomiting. After a couple of hours, Los began to pass his bowels. Yes, yes, yes. He was also started on 15 percent nutrition. He was started off gradually to increase if he did well and keep his nutrition down. I was hoping for success.

My sister-in-law Lovie came to visit early this morning. We chatted awhile and left to go get something to eat and to have a drink, which I could use. My Los Man was holding his nutrition down well, so it had been increased to 40 percent. Yes, God was working, and so was prayer. His room was kept so cold. I was sitting here with my hood on my head and a blanket over my lap. But as long as Los was fine, I was fine. After Lovie left, my friend Beverly came up for a visit. She is a sweet friend and had been showing me and Los much support. Then not long after she left, my mom and Aunt Judy came up for a visit. Judy is very spiritual and always has words of faith to share. When she would visit, I would have her say our prayers with us. She is a wonderful prayer warrior.

Carlos had a bad coughing spell today. He seemed to not be able to lay flat on his back. He coughed and choked hard during his bath. I wanted to tell the nurse to sit him up and forget washing his back. But I held back since she kept apologizing to him, and she was trying to hurry. I think she got a little extra concerned as well. Her name is Kristen. She's a little lady, cute and polite. She told Los to relax and that his mom was right here with him. I appreciate the kindness of the nurses and staff here at Metro. Other than that, he was keeping his nutrition down. So far so good. We would pray for overnight success as we say our prayers before we go to sleep.

September 14, 2017

Carlos made it through the night. They checked on him about every hour to suction him. I didn't think he slept too well, so I didn't wake him too early this morning. As long as I got some form of movement from him, I was good. He showed me little response with his toes, but I knew he was tired.

The doctors made their rounds and said that Carlos was doing good. His nutrition was at 40 percent, and he was receiving it well. Yay, Los, God is great and awesome! We slept in this morning since I was off today. I left for a few hours to run errands and tidy up at home. The air and the break felt good, though I couldn't stop thinking about Los. I felt as if I was leaving a newborn when I leave him.

This morning, Carlos had been having some hard coughing spells. He was sweating from them, yet it was only sixty-six degrees in his room. The nurse had seen that I was nervous and told me that the coughs get better. It was normal. But watching him strain and turn red as he sweated was painful for me. I felt so helpless for him. I tried to soothe him by rubbing his feet and keeping his face wiped, but damn, I was nervous. I patted his chest, wiped the secretions, raised his bed, and prayed for him to get some relief. The nurse cleaned him up and suctioned him. He was good for a few minutes, then he started back up. It was as if he had a cold or was getting sick with something. I sure hoped he didn't catch pneumonia with it being so cold in this room and him sweating. The nurse even put a wet towel on his head. I was not fond of the wet towel since he was already sweating, and his pillow was wet from sweating and had to be turned over. I had found him a dry spot earlier while I waited for the nurse to come.

Well, Carlos was calm for now, so I said our prayers and called it an early night. He didn't respond much with his toes today. I believe all this coughing was wearing him out, so I didn't try to make him respond too much. He gave me a wiggle of the toe once this evening, so that's fine with me. I knew he's tired, so I let him rest. Auntie Cindy came to visit him today. She stayed for a couple of hours. I was going to see if I could find some life insurance for Carlos, at least some term, and pay for it for a year.

Moved from ICU

September 17, 2017

Carlos made it to this day, and he was still here with us. He had been pretty stable over the past couple of days. He was now in room 745, and the staff on this floor was nice. I noticed that Carlos's belly felt plump. His dad said that he knew. They stopped his nutrition again and gave him a suppository to help his bowels. Lord, please don't let him have trouble with his bowels. Also he said that the nurse told him that Carlos had a few spots on his lungs from lying on his back for so long. He was going to get a chair so that he could sit up for a few hours a day to help with the coughing and to prevent him from catching pneumonia.

His dad was going to stay with him this weekend, and he tended to him well and with such a calm voice and care. I'm thankful that he cares for his children so dear. This cough Carlos has was so severe at times that he sat himself up, turned red, and sweated. It ached me so bad to see him like this. I could see how painful it was for him, and I began to feel so bad for him. The cough seemed to have gotten better since Friday, but it was still bad.

I knew it's painful. I didn't make it to see him Saturday because I had to work both jobs, so I called and texted his dad to check on him. He had been coughing and resting all day. No responses of the toes. Oh, but, the nurse tickled his foot and got a reaction, so on Saturday night, after I left work, when I visited Los, I tickled his foot, and yes, he drew back. His cough seemed to have gotten better on Saturday. He didn't cough much at first while I was visiting, but he did soon after. Man, oh man, how I prayed that cough leaves. How much secretions could there be?

Today was a busy day at work for me, my double day. So Carlos and I were going to say our prayers early because I was sleepy, and I was going to watch television until I fall asleep.

September 18, 2017

My Los Man made it through the night, and he had a bowel movement. Yes, yay, Los. He slept well until the nurse disturbed him to check his vitals, changed, and gave him his meds. His coughing had subsided some. He was going to get an x-ray of his stomach to make sure everything is okay. I spoke to his nurse about his swollen cheekbone. At first, she couldn't see the difference, but once she laid him back, she had seen it. She said it might just be swollen because it felt soft. I was still concerned and would ask again.

Well, I had some music playing for Los right now. We started off with some good ole gospel songs of miracles and faith, then today's R&B, rap, or whatever came on the iPad next. He moved his head from side to side a little, blinked with his eyes closed, and his arms were flailing earlier when he coughed. That was different. He's resting right now, and the x-ray nurses were here, so I was going to go home and freshen up as well as get a workout in, then I'd be back.

So I came back, and Los was back from getting his x-ray. He was sleeping well. He had physical therapy today and didn't cough while they had him sitting up. They were trying to get him used to sitting up because they were getting him a special chair. Sitting up a few times a day should help him with bringing up the mucus and to help prevent pneumonia from lying in. He also got therapy on his arms and legs.

I left to go over to my aunt Lena's house. I wasn't gone no more than an hour and a half when I came back to find Carlos's head leaning over. He had a towel on his head and was foaming at the mouth. It was thick and running down his face. I panicked and looked out into the hallway. I saw a male nurse. I asked him if he could help me clean Los up. He said sure, and when he saw Los, I saw he was surprised to see him like that as well. He said, "Well, damn." But he tried to ease my mind by saying that it could have happened within minutes.

I was upset and said, "Well, I don't know how long he's been like this. Where is everyone?"

Before I left, I made sure to clean his throat, soothe him, and let him know that I would be right back. Now all I could do was pat him, rub his head and hands, while I apologized for what he was going through. This made me think of how he was being treated when I was not here. If and when he went to a nursing home, would he be neglected? Lord, I have to really pray before I choose a home to put him in. No one came to visit today, but just as long as I was here, I really didn't care if anyone else came. Life went on for everyone after a few visits.

His brothers didn't come visit him as much as I would like them to. I wondered how they would feel if they were in Los's shoes, and their siblings didn't come to visit them. But I'm here for the long haul. I just had to take care of myself so that I could take care of my Los Man. God, please watch over Carlos when I was not around. Please, Lord! Okay, I would go to sleep or at least lie down and listen out for Los. He tended to cough as soon as I got under the cover. I didn't mind. These nurses on this floor didn't check on him every hour like downstairs. This really made me sad, and tears fell. I felt as if he should be of a higher priority. I felt like I should get paid, ha, ha.

September 19, 2017

Carlos made it through the night. We didn't sleep well because of his coughing. The nurse didn't come to check on him as much as I would've liked, so I was left to do most of his care myself as far as the suctioning, wiping his face, and trying to assure him that he would be okay. I had to leave for work, and my sister-in-law was coming to look after him. The social worker was getting me a list of facilities to research, so I'd check those out today after work, but for now, I was running late. Carlos still hadn't responded to me. I was just a little worried. I hoped it was just because of the coughing wearing him out.

Signs of Awareness

September 20, 2017

Through the grace of God, Carlos was still here. He slept well through the night. His coughing had really gotten better. His eyes opened and blinked more often, especially to discomfort, and he made faces a lot too. Today I felt good as well. I left to go workout as well as freshen up. When I came back, I put some music on and began to lotion down his arms and hands. He was very stiff on his left side and drew back from stretching his arms. I could get him to relax after a few minutes. As I was singing to him, I admired how handsome and rested he looked. I'd sure be glad when he opened those eyes and follow me.

He had therapy today and did well at it. He opened those eyes wide as if to say ouch, wait, whoa when the therapist bent his left leg. He was aware and did respond to pain or discomfort; that's for sure. I also felt as if he was trying to hold my hand when I was exercising his right arm, because his grip got tight.

I'd been drawing Carlos pictures and poems of hope and inspiration. I played music that he liked in hopes that something sparked in his mind. His brothers hadn't been here to visit in over a week. But I was here.

Well, Los and I were going to say our prayers and listen to a gospel song before I lay down for the night. Los was really doing well despite not waking up. He looked so well rested and handsome.

Carlos's dad and I went to look at a facility to place Los this evening, Westpark Neurology and Rehabilitation Center. The place was clean, and the staff was pleasant. It had a really outdated appearance. But overall, it was satisfying. We also went to visit Agartala health care, but they wouldn't let us in, said to come back in the morning. We didn't like the area, so we didn't go back.

I never would've thought that I would be looking for a nursing home to place my twenty-one-year-old son. This whole thing still hadn't sunk in yet. It all felt surreal. I really felt as if I was just going through the motions, and this would end soon. I prayed we could find a place that could handle all his needs. The worker told me that it would be a challenge due to his age and the level of care that he needed. Oh, God, I pray for a place that would truly take care of him.

September 21, 2017

My Los Man had a rough night. He vomited up his nutrition; fever, heart rate, and blood pressure spiked. The trauma doctors were called to check him out, and x-rays were done. After about an hour, he came back down and began to rest better. The tube feed was stopped, and he was given a suppository this morning.

My day was very emotional. I spoke words of strength and faith to him. We listened to Pastor Vernon this morning. His topic was "Prayer Saved My Life," a so well-needed sermon for us. I knew Los was listening because his eyes opened, and he was moving. My heart just ached, and I couldn't help but cry when he had a bad day. My sister-in-law would be here soon so that I could go to work.

The housekeeper this morning was really sweet. She spoke words of faith to us as well. She had seen my tears and said not to worry. "Los is coming out of this, and he is praying inside."

The doctor also said that he was sorry. His nurse for today said that she would treat him as her own. This would get me through the day. Thank you, Lord. I was going to hug the housekeeper because she asked me. I didn't respond when she first asked.

September 26, 2017

Well, Carlos had been pretty stable over the past few days. His coughing had subsided more, and he was sleeping better at night, although last night, he vomited, and I had to call for a nurse. I explained what happened to her, and she said okay. By the time she came back to assist him, I had cleaned him up, changed his bandage and gown. She came back after about an hour. It's a good thing that his dad, my sister-in-law, and myself spent a lot of time here.

There's this home called the Normandy Healthcare, and they were a good fit. My mom, Los's Dad, and I all used to work with the director of nursing there. We all worked at Carnegie Care Center in the 1990s. I felt very confident about Los going there. His dad and his dad's sister were worried about the distance and gas. I didn't care about that as long as he got the care he needed.

I had my daughter and her aunt go to check out Willow Park Convalescent Home on Harvard; it was a no-go. I had to force his dad to look at the list and see if he wanted the liaison to send referrals to any in particular. He looked at the list and said "yeah, those look good," very uninterested. I took the list and asked him if he could put a check next to the ones he was interested in so that I would know which ones to have her send a referral to. So he checked off seven, and they all came back no. I didn't want it to seem as if I was making all the decisions, so I made sure he participated or, at least, had the opportunity to.

His dad and I sat down to discuss the different facilities, and the Normandy was the best fit. When I told my children and his aunt that we chose the Normandy, his dad acted as if he had no idea. He made my sister-in-law feel as if I decided everything on my own, talking about he thought we would make a decision together. I asked him and offered to take him to look at the Normandy, and he said no. I asked why. He said in an irritated tone, "Because I'm tired, Donnie."

I held back my frustration and prayed for strength because this was not a time for this. I asked him if he was coming up to the hospital today, and he said that he hadn't planned on it and asked, "Are you going?" I said, "Yes, I go every day that I can, and I will continue to go no matter where he's at." And then he replied with, "maybe."

Throughout our entire relationship, I had always had to be the decision maker and the one who did all the footwork to make things happen. This I had to explain to my sister-in-law. She said that she just wanted to make sure that his dad was informed. I asked her what made her think that I wouldn't communicate with him when it came to Carlos. She spoke of the guardianship paperwork that had to be filed. I guess she thought I was doing something sneaky; I'm not sure.

I said, "Yes, I'm just doing what I know needs to be done, and I wouldn't do anything without letting his dad know." I was really beginning to feel as if she thought she had more say so than she had, but I didn't have the strength for this type of stuff right now. But anyhow, after a brief disagreement (we were at the hospital, in the lounge area), we hugged, and she said as long as his dad was in agreement, she would step back. She really made me feel as if I was a nonfactor, and she had more control over my son's life decisions than me. I went to Carlos's room feeling very sad and down. I let out a few tears and regained my strength. I really didn't know why he was acting as if he knew nothing. So after his dad and I talked again this evening, the Normandy it was.

Carlos was looking to get transferred today, but the insurance company had to come out and assess him first, so maybe tomorrow. Carlos got his trachea tube changed to a smaller size. It had a pink color to it, the mucus. The nurse said it's normal and would go away. I hope he stopped coughing altogether soon. Well, I was going to take a break for now.

September 27, 2017

My Los Man slept okay last night. The new trachea seemed to be working fine. I had a request to draw a picture of a nurse angel so that it could be hung at the nurses' station in remembrance of Carlos. Well, ask and you shall receive, so I stopped what I was doing and drew her a picture, and I wrote "Nurses are Angels sent from God" at the bottom of the drawing. She was so happy, and she hugged me. I also wrote on the back, "Thank you all for taking care of Carlos. May you all be blessed." Her name is Nurse April.

Today was pretty calm. The neurosurgeon came in and did a test on Los. He said he had progressed well, but he was still at risk for bedsores, infections, pneumonia, etc., so we needed to make sure that the nursing home took care of him. He also said that Los wasn't responding to any commands. I felt as if he came in and out because I could swear that he looked me right in my eyes when I talked to him at times. I was going to hold on to every bit of hope and continue to pray for him and with him. We were in the process of transferring him today, so if all went well, he would be moved to his new home today.

His dad believed that he hit him on the arm. I might have said this already, but oh, well, this is my journal, and I can repeat if I want to. His dad was on his way up, so maybe I could go home and shower while he was here. Oh yeah, the representative from Medicaid came in to assess Carlos, and he said that Carlos should get approved; he just had to submit the paperwork, so that's a plus for today. I was glad I was off from work today and would be for tomorrow too, so I hope he got transferred while I was off. I would like to be with him when he got to his new temporary, short-term home.

The Big Move

September 28, 2017

Today makes one month since Los had been in a coma, and he was still here with us. I thank God for every moment, second, minute, hour, and day that he allowed me to be able to tell Carlos how much we love him. I felt more confident each day Carlos was alive, for I saw a change just about every day. Carlos got transferred to the Normandy Care Center today, and his dad and I were confident about it. I felt a bit of relief, as if he had graduated to his next level of care, and things would be getting better. He just had to let his brain heal a little longer. God was working.

The DON at the Normandy told us that the administrator only accepted Carlos because of her because they don't normally take someone as young as him. So it was sure good to know people in important positions. I hadn't seen, nor spoken to her in over twenty-five years, but my mother kept in touch with her, and she was as excited to see us as we were to see her. She assured me that they would take good care of my son. But I had to ask her again if they would please take care of him. She said that they take good care of all their patients. I said, "I know, I just have to be sure to ask for myself because I'm so nervous, and that's my baby."

My mom rode out to the Normandy with us, and she and the DON talked and caught up on some things. The three of us talked about our children and reminisce about the days when we all worked together. The Normandy is a beautiful place. It has a very nice patio with rocks and flowers, trails and benches, a nice place to sit and read, paint, think, or talk. They even have a mini golf course and a pond with a waterfall. It's so relaxing. What a beautiful landscape. The lobby doesn't have the appearance of a nursing facility. There's beautiful artwork hanging throughout the facility, and we were allowed to personalize Los's room. So of course, I framed his drawings that I did, and they would be getting hung up soon. I was happy about that.

So far so good. Things were falling into place and would only get better through faith and prayer. It was a little hard leaving my Los Man tonight. He looked so comfortable and at ease, as I was as well. Oh, Carlos let out a growl or noise when he yawned. It surprised us because that's the first noise we've heard from him, so that was something new. I'd take it as progress and a little closer to healing.

I said our prayers, and we all said our goodbyes for the night and agreed that we felt good about him being here. Oh, and the hospital sent him with a bedsore. The DON believed it was a stage 2, and she said that they hadn't treated it. The nurses at the Normandy changed the dressing and would evaluate his wounds tomorrow and take care of it. I prayed it would heal well and for Carlos to recover soon.

September 29, 2017

Well, today I went to work at Sweet Melissa, and I got off early, so of course, I went to spend some time with Los, about an hour and a half. I was supposed to work my second job, but I got called off. I was glad about that. I took Los some blankets, a pillow, a hamper, and some socks. When I got to his room, the TV was on a nice music station, and the window was open to let some sunshine in on Los. I hung his get-well cards on his bathroom door, and we listened to music, watched TV, and prayed. I could see that the activities person had visited.

All his caretakers appeared to be very concerned about him. That was so comforting. I was his only visitor today. I bought some pictures to be hung and batteries for the clock in his room. I left around 4:30 p.m. to go to a fundraiser Zumba class at Maple Heights High School. That was fun. The girls were so excited to be live on FB. After Zumba, back to the Normandy to be with Los I went. I left at 11:30 p.m.

More Signs of Awareness

October 5, 2017

It had been a couple days, but Los was still with us. He showed a little something different each day. He was trying to move his head from side to side. He could reposition his arms and only coughed 1–2 times during my visits. The nursing home called me on October 2 at 4:47 a.m. and asked if they could put a catheter on him because his cap catheter came off. I told them that it was okay, then at 6:10 a.m., I got another call from them saying that they couldn't get any urine out, and they caused him to bleed and couldn't stop it, so they needed to send him to the hospital, I said okay. I got another call from them at 7:08 a.m. to let me know that he was at Metro. Through my sleepiness, I was being very calm.

Once I woke up and got out of bed, I had a chance to think. Well, bleeding came from the blood thinners, which made it hard to stop the bleeding. I called the home around noon and asked if Carlos had gotten back yet. The nurse on the phone said he had just gotten back, and she was on her way to check on him. She apologized repeatedly, and I accepted. Good thing I'm pretty understanding. I told her that I would be there soon and hung up, trying not to panic.

One of the physical therapists asked me if I felt as if Carlos followed me at times. I said yes because it felt as if he's looking me right in the eyes when I talked to him sometimes. And she said that she really felt that he was staring at something that she had in her hand and followed her with his eyes. Another nurse said that she felt as if he followed her as well. I would take all of this as he's trying to wake up out of this coma.

Yesterday, the DON said the same thing. She believed he was trying to come out of the coma as well. He also appeared to stare at the TV. One nurse said that she could tell when he was getting tired of them. He would start swinging his arms. We just laughed. My mom, aunt, and I visited yesterday as well as my sister-in-law. She seemed happy to see us. I left before Ciauna could FaceTime Los because I had to drop my mom and aunt off at their homes. I was glad to see that the staff were putting his socks on him. They were what you call fun socks.

Today Carlos slept most of the visit. He appeared to be looking at the TV, but when I went up to him, he closed his eyes. Haha, chump. His dad and I watched *The Avengers* while we were there. It was a nice visit. We both like the Marvel and DC comics. Therapy had been sitting Los up in his chair daily. I gotta come here earlier so that I could see him sitting up. Well, I was waiting on Ciauna to FaceTime us, but in the meantime, we would quote our daily word.

Feeling Lonely and Forgotten

October 11, 2017

Carlos is still here with us, resting and healing. On October 6, my family got together to remember my granddad on his birthday as well as party with my uncle Tony because he was in town for the weekend. Well, that's all fine and good, but I had been thinking about the amount of family support that Los and I were getting, and it's little to none. I felt as if they were treating him like a distant cousin, as if they didn't grow up with him, enjoy sleepovers together and all the family gatherings for his entire life. It really hurt, and they just didn't care. No texts, calls, cards, visits, nothing. Yet they could like my posts and updates on FB about him. They could get to anywhere they wanted, but they couldn't get to the nursing home, nor call to check on Los.

So during their festivities, I sent this text to twelve of my family members, including his brothers:

Hello family,

I just want to say that as many family members Los and I have here in Cleveland, your support sucks. You can get together and celebrate death, but you can't get together and uplift and support a young man that's fighting for his life. So with that said, you all can keep your fake thoughts, prayers, and unseen support. Good thing we have God on our side, and you can forget about us. Oh, you already have. Love you anyway because God said I have to.

That summed up how I felt. Some understood, and some didn't. I got a phone call from some, but I didn't answer. I got texts from others. Some I responded to, others I told to save their data; no replies needed. But I was over it now. Oh, my uncle Dale snuck in to visit on October 9, but he didn't tell me, haha, and my uncle Tony.

Since he'd been here at the Normandy, I really haven't had any problems, but I noticed that the aides were not checking on him as much. Yesterday, my sister-in-law was telling the nurse that she had been there for three hours, and no one had come to turn him, and that was at 7:00 p.m., so the nurse sent two aides to his room to turn him. When I left at 9:30 p.m., I noticed that no one had been back to turn him again, so when I got in my car, I called to let the nurse know, and she said that she would get on them.

On October 8, his brother Chaz came to visit. It's sad that I had to send out a text to get their attention, but it worked. It was very hard on Chaz and Chuck to see him this way, but it was even harder for Los to be that way, so I tried to be understanding and patient, but they needed to make a better effort. You never knew whose voice would spark a reaction out of him.

I was here visiting Los today before I went to work at 4:00 p.m., so I had to leave here at 3:30 p.m. I didn't know if I could make it back tonight, so I came before work. I missed him so much when I didn't see him, and my day wouldn't go well at all. The nurse just changed and turned him. I helped her pull him up. I felt better about leaving him once I saw him, so until later. Bye, Los.

All Is Well

October 25, 2017

Well, I guess reporting Carlos's progress later and later was a good thing as far as there were no problems. Since I had last written about my Los Man, he had caught an infection in his trachea and was on antibiotics. His orthopedic appointment was canceled and rescheduled for today, but when I got to the hospital, it had been canceled again. Someone failed to notify me. Carlos's nurse told me that his pillow had fallen behind the bed, and when she went to pick it up, he was sitting up. She said that she didn't sit him up, so he did that on his own, then she put the pillow behind his head, and he lay back. She said she was tickled about that, and all she could do was say, "All right, Mr. Carlos." He had also let out a yell while a nurse was in his room. She said it scared her. I had heard him do that before when he had a big yawn.

He had visitors more often. I picked up my aunts Lena and Cindy almost weekly, and Monday, my cousin came as well. One of my sisters-in-law came out a couple of days ago while I was here. It was nice seeing her.

Carlos was still focusing on us at times. He drew back his feet when I tickled them. The therapist said it's reflex. I thought otherwise because he only did it when I touched his foot. He had also been biting his bottom lip, and it's swollen up big. The nurse thought that he was trying to communicate pain or something, so they'd been giving him Tylenol. She said it's helping a little. I talked to Los and told him that he needed to stop biting his lip because I didn't want him to cause too much damage. I hoped he heard me. I felt so bad anytime something happened to him. He bit his lip while I was talking to him. I had to pry his mouth open to get his lip out. It scared his dad and grandma. I really hoped he stopped doing that because he has nice lips.

According to his nurse, he didn't sleep much at night. She said when she checked on him, his eyes were wide open. The staff kept the TV on programs like football, music, and even had it on the music awards where he appeared to be watching it. Well, I was about to start another painting before I left tonight, so until next time. I prayed all went well with my Los Man.

October 27, 2017

My Los Man was still fighting. He responded so well to me on the twenty-fifth that I videoed it and posted it to FB. Every time I asked him to move his toes, he did. Even a tiny bit made me so happy and proud of him. Today, I was carving him a pumpkin for his room. I did it while on FB Live. It took about an hour. I had quite a few people watching as I talked and carved. It was fun.

Carlos had a white film on his tongue because he wouldn't open his mouth for cleaning. So he had been put on an oral medication to get rid of it. I hope it worked. Well, they said it should. He bit his lip again after it had just healed up so well, but I caught it just in time, so no marks. Yay! He also coughed up a big yuck. I hadn't seen that in a while. I hope it was just the infection clearing up. He looked so well rested today. I wondered if he knew I was carving a pumpkin. He used to love doing this together. I did tell him what I was doing.

My Los Man was sleeping a lot lately. Maybe he is a night owl and wakes up in the wee hours of the night. Well, I had rubbed and put lotion on his feet, so now I guess I'd call it a night after we said our prayers and thank God first.

Bad News

October 30, 2017

Carlos is still here, healing and resting. Last night he reacted very well to his dad's voice. He moved his whole foot for Ciauna. That made her cry. She said that it made her very happy as well as sad. I told her I know it's hard, and I understood, but we had to find the joy in it all. His reaction made us all so excited, and I knew that God was working on him.

I thought about the date. On October 28, it had been two months since Carlos had been in a coma. Ciauna was surprised and didn't feel as if it had been two months already.

I said, "No, I feel like it's been two months, though time is going by. I'm hoping that Los give me the best Christmas present this year by waking up."

He received a letter from the state today. It said that he was being charged with vehicular homicide. What a blow to myself. Although I knew these were not my personal charges, his dad and I felt so terrible for him. Carlos had no idea of what's going on, nor the challenges he had to face in the future. This news stole my happiness, and I got out of the mood to go shopping.

With the heart that Los has, I knew that this would be hard for him to accept. My heart ached for him so badly, but I had to stay strong so that I could continue to encourage him with hope, faith, and strength. I tried to speak positivity into him always. Well, I guess I'd surf the web and then paint to get my mind at ease for a moment.

November 5, 2017

Today my Los Man is still here resting well. He might have another infection, but I hoped not. Yesterday when I asked him if he wanted to talk to Ciauna on the phone, his eyes went straight to the phone, and he focused on her. I knew he heard and understood us. He just couldn't respond with words. He stayed awake almost the entire hour that I was here, and we were talking to him. God is so good. Chaz came up to visit for a good period of time yesterday as well. Chaz sounded a little sad but okay overall. He was taking this hard.

I'd been trying not to worry about Carlos's future and focused on the now, so I'd continue to take it day by day. I knew things would fall in place and go according to God's will and his only. Pray, pray, pray, and keep the faith I shall. I felt strongly about him waking up. He just had to heal a bit more. My family and friends gave me words of encouragement and faith. It helped most times.

Today I had a moment of crying, so I put my fingers to work and played some gospel music on my phone. Now that made me feel much better. I came out to see Los in a bad thunderstorm today. His dad was already there. We FaceTimed Ciauna for a good while, had a few laughs, and snacked on some Greek pastries that I had brought home from a Greek wedding that I worked the night before. I thought that I was going to paint while I was here, but it was getting late. Well, maybe I would get an hour in or just finish watching *Thor* with Los. Yeah, that's what I'd do. So until later. Oh, wait, I met a new aide today that was taking care of Los. His name was Enoch, and I recognized it from the Bible. He was very caring.

Back to the Hospital

November 20, 2017

Wow, I didn't realize so many days had gone by. My Los Man was still with us and fighting hard. Since the last few weeks, Carlos had spent three days in the hospital due to coughing his trachea out. He had to be kept because his blood pressure was high, heartbeat was faster than normal, had fever, and still fighting an infection. The Normandy called me at 4:30 a.m. and told me that he needed to go to emergency because they couldn't replace his trachea, then again at 5:00 a.m. to ask me if it was okay to take him to Fairview Hospital. Then Fairview Hospital called me to ask if it was okay to treat him.

I went to visit Los later that day at the Normandy and came to find out that he was admitted to the hospital. That was shocking and scary. The nurse called Fairview so that I could talk to the nurse, and she assured me that Los was fine. I didn't see him for three days due to work. I did good until day two and a half; I started to worry.

Carlos came back that following Sunday and had quite a few visitors that day. His friends, grandma, aunts, and cousins, my uncle Jr. had visited him at the hospital. Los had a smaller trachea, and he no

55

longer used a catheter. It was so great that he could move his bowels and urinate on his own. He also focused more.

Last night, Ciauna had a moment. She called me crying because she was sending out her wedding announcements, and she said that Los wouldn't be able to be in her wedding. I told her not to think like that and don't count Carlos out because he would be in her wedding. "Whether it be in a wheelchair or walking, he's going down that aisle. Carlos wouldn't miss that, and besides, he has a whole year to get ready. A lot can change by then. So send him his gift, and I will read his card to him."

She said thanks and felt much better. We talked a little more, and holding back my tears was hard. Trying to stay strong and faithful for myself and others is hard but necessary. She said it was hard for her, and I said it was hard for me as well. As much as I liked seeing him sit up in the chair, it made me sad because he slumped and couldn't sit up straight. But he would in time. I was hopeful of that.

Well, it's almost Thanksgiving, and the Normandy had dinner for the residents, and two family members per resident could attend. I couldn't get the day off, so my sister-in-law took my place. When I got off work, I was pooped. I slept four hours and didn't make it to see Los because it was late, and I couldn't get myself together. Sometimes what he was going through just overwhelmed me, and I couldn't stop crying. I had also painted two pictures since then.

Trying to Keep My Life Together

December 9, 2017

My Los Man was still resting and healing. It had been a while since I wrote but only due to my emotions, work, and moving into my new home. Since the last time I wrote, my days had been pretty emotional. On Thanksgiving Eve, I woke up with Los on my mind, and I wept and was sad the entire day. I prayed, listened to gospel music, and a sermon from Joyce Meyer, I called my aunt Judy so that we could pray. Some days were better than others. This holiday season was really getting to me. I had a moment while I was moving, so I called his dad, and we talked. He knew just what I was thinking. I was thinking of how Carlos would've been the first to help me move, take charge, and show me how strong he was by carrying the biggest and heaviest boxes. He liked to show me his strength, and I enjoyed seeing it. I knew when he woke up he would show me how strong he was when it came to therapy. I'd be his number one cheerleader.

My heart ached so much for him. I spoke to the girl's mom on Thanksgiving Eve but was unable to speak much. We were both having a bad day. My cousin Buster also called and spoke some words of encouragement to me. I thank God for those who reached out to me with genuine concern here on earth. For I know my true strength comes from the heavens. Carlos lost some weight, and his knees were showing.

They looked big and knobby. So his feeding had been increased so that he could gain some weight. His dad kept his hair cut, and he looked so handsome.

Christmas would be here in two weeks. Wow, time seemed to be flying by at times, but then I counted the days, and it had been almost four months for my Los Man. But he was still here, and for that I was thankful. Carlos's cousin Dejuan came to see him. I didn't know his reaction when he had seen Los, but I was sure he was sad. They were very close and only two weeks apart in age. Dejuan didn't take the news about him well. I knew he was sad to see Carlos in this state.

I woke up around 3:00 a.m. with Los on my mind this past Friday. I tossed and turned, sang gospel songs, and tried to go back to sleep at 4:30 a.m. I just wept so hard. The image of Los lying helpless just kept taking over my mind. I texted his dad and my children to tell them about my morning. Chaz said that he was feeling the same a couple of days ago and wondered if anyone else had those days. I told him yes and often. I was glad he shared that with me, and now he knew that he was not alone. I'd share with him more often. I guess I forgot that he was feeling awful as well. Charles and Ciauna replied with kind words of encouragement.

My aunt Lena and I decorated Carlos's room for Christmas. It looked nice. I also texted my friend telling him about my bad day, and he said that I needed to talk to God and tell him how mad I was and also read, look into Psalms, and find strength because it was important. So I listened to Psalms on audio, and yes, it did help. I didn't feel comfortable expressing my anger to God, but I tried. I felt out of place and couldn't think of what to say.

Carlos was beginning to make more sounds. He coughed from his mouth, and it was loud. He also yawned loud. I believe it was all progress, no matter how small. I also knew that there was something to be learned from all this. So God would reveal everything in his own time.

Tragedy Strikes Again

December 18, 2017

Oh my Lord, tragedy struck my family again, but my Los Man is still here resting and healing. Thank God. So my cousin, she's twenty-seven years old, was in a car accident two Sundays ago. She lost control of the car and hit a tree. She was in a coma and unresponsive. The strange part of this is that she is the daughter of one of my uncles. He and I are two months apart, and so are our firstborn. She is his firstborn. When he and I were around six years of age, we were hit by a car together. Wow, yeah, I know. Now our children had been in car accidents with head injuries and facing the same fate. We both know that God holds the last word, so we were staying strong and hopeful as well as prayerful. My uncle asked if I would draw an angel for her room; of course, I will.

I was sitting here with Los playing holiday music, while Ciauna talked to him. She was showing him how to cook chicken. It was hard for her to look at him for the first few weeks. I used to put the phone to his ear and let her talk to him; now they FaceTime. They love each other so much. I had been feeling better over the past few weeks, trying to get some holiday spirit. I did put my tree up and decorated my house a little. Now I needed to get back to my workouts ASAP.

I always reminded myself that this world is not my home, I thought of how glad I would be when it was over, for I pray to be heaven bound. The pain, famine, wars, and tragedy are getting worse each day in this cruel world. I pray that 2018 would be a better year for us all. A Christmas miracle would be nice. My wish would be for Carlos to wake up and recognize me. But his resting and healing was more important, so patience it is.

Oh, and Carlos had a bad episode last week after talking to Ciauna. He began trying to sit up and kept holding his breath. He was almost sent to the ER. His blood pressure and heart rate rose. He was given Tylenol which appeared to help. His dad was there with him. Thank God for that. I started painting and ran out of white, so I had to stop. I hoped Los was enjoying the holiday music. He seemed to be. Well, I was going to call it a night for now, but I'd be back soon.

December 25, 2017

It's Christmas Day, and my Los Man was still with us resting and healing. Thank God! Carlos had quite a few visitors today. He had been doing good over the past few days. The speech therapist was working with him, and he tracked for her well. He looked to the left, right, and up. When asked to look to the right, he turned his head with it. I asked the therapist if she could ask him to look to the left, and after a few times of us calling his name, he turned his head all the way to the left as he sat up. We smiled and clapped with so much excitement as if he was two years old. That was such a heartfelt moment for everyone in the room. God was showing us his miracle hand.

The Cavs basketball game was on, and Los seemed to be watching it at times. He was showing some interaction with us. He was resting less each day, or should I say staying awake more often. He also focused and tracked more as well. After the visit, we were going to my house for dinner. Maybe I'd call Chaz to see if he wanted to come. My Los

Man was trying to move his legs more. His feet moved more often. He was trying hard, but he got tired after a while and drifted off to sleep or stared off blankly. His cousin Dejuan was holding a mirror to Los's face to see if he recognized himself. Well, he said he did. Okay.

We Made It

December 31, 2017

Okay, it's the last day of the year, and I was with my Los Man to bring in 2018 together. His dad would be here soon to join us. Carlos was sweating a lot when I got here today. His gown was soaked. So I changed his gown, brushed his hair, sat him up, and soothed him to make him comfortable. I had the *Dick Clark* New Year's Eve celebration on TV for us to watch as we chatted.

He looked at the TV periodically, so I believe he was aware of what's going on in that moment, then he drifted off to sleep or stared off blankly. The aide just informed that Carlos didn't get therapy outside of his room any longer. That was surprising to me. I needed to find out why. So my mind was thrown off at the moment. His dad said that the Hoyer lift wasn't working properly. I didn't agree with that reason because his legs and arms were very stiff and needed the therapy.

Well, Carlos made it to 2018. He was showing signs of progress and hope! We thank you, Lord. We thank you, Lord. We thank you, Lord. May Carlos continue to improve, and our faith shall only get stronger from this point on.

Earlier today while at work at Sweet Melissa's, a customer came in today and she gave me two wooden coins along with my tip when she paid for her meal. One had the word *trust* written on one side of it and "Trust in the Lord with all your heart on the other side." The second coin said "John 3:16" on one side and a cross on the other side. She said that the coins kept falling out of her purse all that day, and they fell out in the car on her way to the restaurant. She felt as if they were meant for someone in here. When she told me that, I choked up; and with hesitation, I told her about what I was going through and she was shocked and said, "They must've been for you." We praised God and I felt Holy Spirit's presence. After my shift was over, I was told by my manager that Sweet Melissa's was closing its doors for good. I was shocked. I thought, "How could my year start off like this?" I had just moved to a new house, and now I'm out of a job. I thought of the coins and read them again. God knew what was going to happen, so he sent me a word of encouragement. My heart was so heavy. I wondered how much did God think I could handle because I felt as if I was about to explode. This was one of many ways God would start communicating with me throughout this season.

January 4, 2018

Yep, it's a new year, and my Los Man is still here with us. After his big day on Christmas, he had been sleeping a lot. I thought that took a lot of effort and wore him out. He started to move his leg and his foot on his left side more; it looked as if he was trying to stretch out. I decorated his board and window sill for the new year. I enjoyed decorating his room according to the seasons and holidays. I posted a picture of Carlos's activity board on FB saying "Happy New Year" from Carlos and "thanks for the continued prayers." Some of his friends tried to keep up with his status, so I tried to post an update monthly.

As I sat here, Carlos's leg and arm were moving uncontrollably, I thought. I would love to know if it was intentional, but I couldn't really say because he was asleep as they were moving. He also had a moment today where he was breathing very heavily for 30–45 seconds. Maybe he was having spasms. He also had a strong cough. I had to encourage him to let the cough out. After the third try, he did.

Well, it was getting late, so I rubbed his feet, fed him some gospel, and spoke a few words of encouragement into him. So until later. I'm wrapping it up for tonight. Oh, he has a care conference for tomorrow, so hopefully it all goes well.

January 10, 2018

My Los Man is still here resting and healing. Yes, my God is good! The care conference went well. Carlos had gained one pound this week. The dietician was working on solutions to keep him from losing weight. She said some of the weight loss could be due to the sweating and contractions which burn calories. His therapist agreed that he was tracking more. Another therapist believed that he played possum when he didn't want to be bothered, hahaha. He did close his eyes at the drop of a hat just when you thought he was about to wake up for you.

He was still sleeping a lot since Christmas. Maybe he needed to rejuvenate his mind. He had spasms more in his legs. The nurse had him sitting in a chair, and his legs were straight when he was in the chair, unlike when in the bed, he was in a fetal position. I noticed some gunk in his eyes. I hope it was nothing, but I would let the nurse know so that it could get checked. Carlos opened his eyes and gave me 3–4 looks, right at me in between blinks. He was trying to stay focused. It's as if he heard me calling his name and talking to him, but he just couldn't stay awake.

He seemed to be becoming aware right now. His eyes were wide open, and he was trying to move. Now he was drifting back off to sleep, so I would wrap it up for today and come back tomorrow.

Oh, What a Surprise

January 21, 2018

My Los Man was still resting, healing and fighting to get better. Yesterday, his sister was talking to him, asking him to open his eyes. He started raising his eyebrows. Ciauna and I got so excited. She kept encouraging him to open them, and after a few moments, he opened them. He focused on her face for a few seconds before falling back to sleep. As my aunt Cindy and I began to leave from our visit, I noticed Carlos looking at us as we were leaving. I turned back around to ask him if he was watching us, and I could tell by the look in his eyes that he was saying yes. I was so proud of him and his progress. God was truly working on his healing.

Today my mom, Charles, and I were here visiting Carlos, and when his dad called his name to wake him up, he started opening his eyes and focused on his dad as he talked to him. His dad had the biggest smile as Carlos focused on him. This was the first time he showed his dad that he heard him and focused on him for 30–40 seconds at a time before he lost focus and drifted off to sleep. I was so happy for his dad.

Seeing the different movements and progress, no matter how small, just thrilled us all. The small bits of progress was God showing us his miraculous hands. We appreciated every bit of it. I rubbed his hands and feet for him. It seemed to relax him. He just had his bath for the night, so I was going to let Ciauna speak to him, and then I would be going home.

February 10, 2018

My Los Man was still resting and fighting. He had these muscle spasms and trembled often today. He had fallen out of the bed. *Wow!* I believe the trembles and spasms were so strong that maybe his legs fell over the side of the bed. He was sent to the ER to be checked out, and everything came back good.

His dad got a letter from job and family services stating that Carlos would no longer be receiving medical coverage for his long-term care. What a shock! We couldn't afford to pay for his health care, so hopefully, this was a mistake.

Carlos had been getting visitors regularly, and the support was much appreciated. These shakes he had scared Ciauna and I, although we knew it was him trying and the healing process. It was hard to see him going through this. I could feel his confusion, and I ached for him. At times I couldn't bear to watch him, but I found the strength with God's help and my faith.

Today Carlos was having frequent trembles. It woke him up as soon as he got to sleep good. I hoped he wasn't in pain. He broke out into a sweat and soaked his clothes. I wished there was something that could be done for the trembles. His cousin Buster came to visit him. I wondered if he recognized his voice or if he looked at him.

Well, a friend of mine told me that I was chosen, not sure for what or why. But my strength, courage, and faith in Jesus is no secret. Being strong for others is much easier for me. Sometimes it feels as if people don't expect for strong people or people that they consider strong, to hurt. It's very hard to stay positive around negativity. That's the grace of the Lord shining on me, so I'll stay strong and humble.

February 19, 2018

Carlos is still here with us, resting and healing with the Lord's help. Just as I was rubbing Carlos's feet and legs, I was about to ask him if he was going to give me anything, and he stretched his right leg out fully.

I said, "Oh my god, that is so great." Just as I began to ask, God showed me his work to keep me strong. Also as I wiped his eyes, he squinted harder than ever. He usually just closed his eyes when I touched his face, so that was different, and that was progress.

A couple days ago, Carlos's dad came in his room, and Carlos's legs were hanging over the side of the bed as if he was trying to get out of the bed. He was sliding to the floor. His dad took a picture and showed it to the nurse. We thought that was how he fell out of the bed before. Thank God his dad came in and caught him before he hit the floor.

I was playing this hip-hop gospel radio on Pandora. He opened his eyes periodically as if he heard something in the music. He was pretty aware today, and that made me feel better knowing that his mind was coming more and more alive. Ciauna got a chance to talk to him during her lunch break. She was excited. Well, these eyes were getting sleepy, so I would go get a ten-minute nap. Until next time, bye.

March 7, 2018

My Los Man is still here resting and healing. I hadn't seen him in a week due to work and visiting Ciauna in Texas for my birthday. Carlos had been doing great. Thanks to our Lord and Savior Jesus Christ. He was becoming more alert each day. Today as I rubbed his feet, he pulled back strongly, so I knew he felt me, and I was glad about it.

The Lord called my cousin home, and my heart ached for her mom and my uncle as well as for her children and siblings. I couldn't help but think about Los. And if he didn't make it, I prayed for strength and courage.

Carlos's muscle relaxers had been reduced. His dad and I felt as if they made him too sleepy, although he'd been asleep my entire visit today. The staff said that they had been taking Los out of his room to sit in the lobby more often. He seemed to like it, I guess. Either way, it was great that they got him out. He didn't wear the braces on his hands too much anymore because his hands sweat, and the skin rubbed off his hands and made scars. He still had the trembles, and he was having one right at this moment. His eyes were wide open. Well, I gotta go. It's time to get ready for work, and I was so sleepy. Well, until next time.

Gaining More Awareness

March 21, 2018

My Los Man is still here with us resting, healing and fighting. On March 17, he had a lot of visitors that day—my aunties, uncle, cousin, nephew, and sister. We tried to get him to wake up for us, but I guess he was too tired. He tried though. This was a very great and awesome day.

Over the past few weeks, Carlos had fallen out of the bed again. I really believed it was due to him becoming aware and trying to move his arms and legs. He didn't realize that he didn't have control over his body. But I claimed in Jesus's name that he would regain control over his limbs again, for our Lord has a plan for Carlos, and he wanted him to complete it.

Today Carlos was very active. He was wide awake, making faces as if he had just seen something—shock, concentrated looks of confusion and attempts. His arms and legs were moving a lot, then he drifted off for a minute or two, and then he was back at it. He stretched his legs out more while knocking his pillows, socks, covers, and whatever else was on his bed off onto the floor. I could just imagine how he fell out of the bed. I had pulled him up more than once already.

My Los Man was showing signs of progress each day. I went to touch his face, and he flinched with fear as if I scared him. Um, well, yes, I scared him. He woke up in spurts where he looked so shocked that he appeared to stop breathing. But I believe that was just him trying to respond to what's going on as well as trying to figure this all out.

Well, this was a short visit today, and I didn't want to leave because he was the most active today than he had been in a while. He had many different reactions and responses today. I just wanted to sit and observe every movement that God was allowing him to perform.

May 10, 2018

I was so scared and overwhelmed this past month with all that had been going on. Finding a new job, Carlos fighting infections, in and out of the hospital, not sure if he would make it to his birthday. I prayed and cried almost daily, the enemy had me doubting Carlos's healing, I prayed and spent a lot of time in my prayer closet, asking God to help my unbelief. I felt so helpless and alone as if no one understood what I was going through. This fight was so hard. I was so broken, my smile was gone, and I was just living on autopilot. I had to be strong around everyone so that they didn't feel bad because that would only make me feel worse. So I wore a mask and cried in secret. All the while I attended church twice a week and never told them. I didn't want the pity and all of the suggestions to go along with it. I wanted God to lead and guide me, so I soaked myself in him.

Today is Carlos's birthday, and yes, he is still here with us. He made it to twenty-two. His dad brought some of his friends to visit him for his birthday. Some family members came as well. We bought balloons, presents, and decorated his room. There was a nice amount of visitors that came out for him. I sang happy birthday to him as I did every year. I remember the one year that I didn't sing to him, he asked me why I didn't sing it. I said, "I didn't think you cared. You are like sixteen now."

He said, "But that's what you and Auntie Vira always do." So I sang it then and every year afterward. We had a really good visit, and I was so happy that God allowed him to make it another year. When I asked Holy Spirit if he was going to make it to his birthday, he said yes. But I was battling with doubt. I made a video of the many stages of Carlos playing to the song "Still Here" by the Williams Brothers. My god, it was so hard to do. I cried the whole time that I was making it. It was so beautiful. I posted it to Facebook for all of his friends to wish him a happy birthday.

God Spoke to Me

May 20, 2018

I'd recently had two dreams, well, a dream and a vision. I was still unsure which is which, so I was still trying to discern the difference between dreams, visions, and revelations. In this past week, I dreamt that I went into my grandmother's bedroom, and my daughter, Ciauna, was asleep under the covers. She was fully grown at this point. I was deciding on making the room my craft room because it was bigger. Then the next thing I knew, my aunt and I were on our way to the mall. She was riding a scooter, and I had a moped. She had just gotten her scooter as a gift from her son, I believe. We were riding and just having fun when she made a wrong turn. I went to get her, and as she came around the corner, she looked dazed and demonic. She was babbling and made no sense and didn't recognize me. There were four or five people with her, and they had the same look on their faces.

I grabbed her and tried to persuade her to come with me, and she resisted. Her eyes were all white with just a black speck and a blank stare. I ran because the demons were beginning to come after me.

In the dream I was afraid. This dream was so clear and felt so real. I ended up at a house where this woman let me in. She was kind to me, soft-spoken, with few words. Somehow she ended up doing laundry, and it consisted of my clothes and hers as well. I remember her holding up a pair of panties, and I said they weren't mine. I stated that I was trying to get to the hotel, and her husband said that he was not going to let me leave his wife alone. I tried to leave, but he stopped me. I noticed another lady there, and she started out kind. When I realized that these people were not going to allow me to leave, I began to cry and said over and over that I just wanted to go home. The second lady began to mock me and laugh.

I heard my moped startup outside, so I broke out of the house to see what was going on. A small boy was stealing my moped, and I began to chase him. I noticed my aunt chasing a bigger boy as he rode off on her scooter. I yelled after the smaller boy, and when I caught up to him, I didn't see my moped. It appeared to be about 6:00 p.m. in the evening. I released the boy and went back into the house. Later that evening closer to sunrise, I heard my moped again. It was the same boy. This time I retrieved my moped and took it into the house with me.

When I was chasing the boy, we were running through snow, yet I wasn't cold, nor could I recall having on winter outerwear. But this was all a dream, so I just went with it.

I noticed two policemen walking down the street, so I started to run and yelled toward them, trying to get their attention. The husband began to chase me. He caught me and covered my mouth. I got away and yelled, "Help!" The husband started yelling also to drown me out. The husband then ran in the opposite direction and yelled for someone to light a cherry bomb to distract the policemen.

I could see the policemen walking toward a car. It looked as if a man was slumped over in the car or under it. As I got closer to the policemen, they disappeared. I kept running, and I ended up cradling the man at the car. And my dream ended. I woke up with a feeling of panic and fright.

The dream was disturbing to me, so I got up to use the bathroom, and while sitting there, I asked God, "What was going on with this dream? What did it mean? This is a bit much. Please tell me what's going on." In the midst of my questions, God said Matthew 13. I looked around and said to myself, *Matthew 13*. I was so shocked to have heard that. God said read. I went to get my iPad, and God said, "your Bible." So I said okay with a bit of shock because I discerned his voice almost instantly.

I read Matthew 13 and got my answer after verse 10, I believe, but I read the entire chapter anyway. It talks about seeds being sown and planted and good seeds being picked from among the bad seeds.

What I got out of this, with the help of a friend, was that Jesus has been with me all my life, keeping me from the bad people. Only he can save me. No one else. He is revealing to me that there are people who meant me no good, while showing me myself and that I'm a protector. It came to me that the man that was injured in the car was my son Carlos. I felt that knowing so strongly as I elaborated on the passage that I read.

There was another part of this dream I'd just recalled. I ran across the street to a house, and my sister-in-law opened the door. There were two small children there as well. I asked her to call me an Uber because I had left my cell phone at the hotel, and I needed to go back there and get it. She grabbed the yellow pages and began to look through the movie section.

I told her, "That's not how you find an Uber." She insisted that she knew what she was doing. I eventually left after a few more attempts to get her to find me an Uber.

I felt so good being obedient to God and discerning his voice when he answered my question. I was a little shocked that he answered so quickly. Well, he has always answered me; I just didn't listen as much as I should have. After this dream, I realized that God was telling me Carlos was in trouble and would be okay because soon after, he got sick again.

A few days later, I had a vision of a man driving a bus. He was of black complexion, with white hair, crew cut, had a mustache and beard, quite handsome in appearance and wore a pleasant smile. He told me "bye" as I was getting off the bus, and I told him to have a great day. I asked God who he was, and Jesus came to mind. Yet I knew that Jesus died at the age of thirty-three, and I didn't think that Jesus had white hair. Maybe the man's presence was loving like Jesus. I didn't want to doubt God, so I would wait on more clarity and see if I would see this man again one day.

I'm sure that I will have more dreams, visions, and revelations as God continues to break and mold me. I know he is doing all this for my good. Last night, I sat in bed with my legs crossed and my hands clasped to pray. As I began to pray, Holy Spirit filled my body, and I wept as I prayed. The feeling was awesome.

Setbacks, Pain, and Blessings

May 24, 2018

Today I was filled with so much emotion. My heart was heavy, and my eyes wouldn't stop crying. I felt as if my faith was being tested. I wouldn't ever stop believing in the Lord my God. I was once told to tell God how mad I was; that didn't feel right to me. I can't bear to be mad at God, for if he can give me triumphs, so why not trials and tribulations? I will always withstand whatever God allows to come my way for I know he will be with me to see me through it all, though sometimes I may feel sad, and my heart may be troubled.

The reason I felt this way today is because Carlos was in the ICU unit at Fairview Hospital. His blood count was down, and he needed a blood transfusion.

God said that he would be okay, and I believed that. I just couldn't help the worrying. Well, I was not sure if it was worry or doubt. At times I do feel a speck of doubt and surely didn't want to doubt God by any means. I shall pass this test of faith, and Carlos would be just fine.

God asked Ezekiel if these bones could live. So when I saw Carlos, I was reminded of that, and I said, "Yes, these bones can live, and they will." I felt as if I had more power of the Spirit in me than I was willing to admit or experience. This was where my unbelief came in, and God wanted me to believe wholeheartedly. I prayed that these chains on me be broken all the way because though they were broken, there were still a link or two holding on.

I prayed and was listening and singing to some great gospel music. Some of the songs were touching me so deep that I couldn't help but cry. God's Spirit got into me, and I was lost for words, so the tears did the talking for me. I often think of my grandmother's strength during these times.

I told one of my coworkers about a dream of water that I had and how I was blessed with money by someone afterward. This had happened several times after I had a dream of falling water. She said that she asked God for water to be thrown on her, and she said that God told her that she hasn't gone through what I have or will. She said that dreams of water is good. Yet that statement, I pondered in my mind. I told her that I didn't feel as if I was going through anything, no different than anyone else; it's just life. She said I might feel as if it was nothing, but it is. I only wondered how much more I could handle because right now, this heart of mine was heavy, and I just didn't know what to expect next, but I would face it. I'd never give up.

At this moment, all I could do was rock, cry, and listen to the music telling me I am his own, and he knows my name. The worries of my son and finances were so overwhelming, yet I was asked by a stranger if I could get him something to eat yesterday. I was leaving Auto Zone because my car needed wheel hub bearings, which I was trying to see how I could afford them. The man said that he had just left the hospital, Metro, and was put on a soft food diet and could eat mashed potatoes. There was a KFC next door, so I drove over through the drive-through window and ordered him a large serving of mashed potatoes. He proceeded to ask for help with getting his meds as he said thank you. I said no because I felt as if he was pushing my kindness.

But God made me with love and care, so through it all, I had to share what I have for the love of God, even while facing my own trials and tribulations. I know God lives in me, and he only wants me to let him shine fully through me as I touch others. This road is rocky, "but Lord, don't take away my stumbling blocks; just lead me all around." This is a verse taken from one of my grandmother's favorite songs, "Lord Don't Move My Mountain."

God Speaks Through Dreams

May 26, 2018

Today I felt so much better. Carlos was doing better. I drove my friend to his weight competition, and during the break, I took a nap in my car. I had a dream. My sister, sister-in-law, my grandchild, and myself were all at a hotel, and there was a pool there that they wanted to get in. I didn't like the pool because it was dirty. So my sister and sister-in-law got into the pool anyway. I told my grandchild that she couldn't get into that dirty water. She tried, and I caught her and scolded her again. I turned my head, and when I turned back to look at her, she was at the bottom of the pool. I myself can't swim, and neither could she.

I was yelling, "Get her out. She's right there." After I had searched for what looked like several minutes, I was yelling with panic. "She's right here. Get her out." Someone reached out the hand of a child to me. As I pulled the child up, I noticed it wasn't her. I put that child to the side and pointed to the water. "That's her." And I grabbed her hand, pulled her out, and lay her flat on the ground. I pumped her chest twice; water came out from her mouth. I lifted her up into a sitting position and held her as I thanked God over and over, Thank you, Lord. Thank you, Lord.

I awoke to my friend tapping on the car window.

This dream stayed on my mind, and I asked God what's the meaning. "Research," he said, so I looked up the meaning of water in dreams. It answered some of my questions, and it did relate to some of what I was going through in my dreams. I can relate to crying as to mean cleansing of one's self. I myself always relate water as having something to do with a blessing of money.

May 30, 2018

God answered my dream that I had about my grandchild.

June 4, 2018

Oh, what a glorious feeling I was possessing in my mind, body, and spirit. So I met this woman Friday while I was at work at the embassy. She was a customer. We first started talking about the Cavaliers basketball game, then politics, and how it relates to religion. She told me that she felt the strong presence of God in me. I told her, "Well, yes, he is with me, and he must think that I am very strong because what I'm going through is a lot." She said, "No, honey, God is carrying you." Again I said very nonchalantly, "Yes, I know."

She said that Holy Spirit told her that God had something very great, great for me, and that she had never heard two *greats* together before, so it must be something special. That made my heart smile. As we kept conversing, she did a little shake of her head and shoulders as if Holy Spirit was upon her. I could feel the Holy Spirit with us. This let me know that she is a woman of God. I told her about Carlos, and she seemed surprised. She said that she would never have known because I was singing and working as if everything was okay. I said, "God has me and him, so I'm okay, yet my heart is aching."

She told me that she used to minister to the lawyers and congressmen on Capitol Hill. She's from Virginia, married with one son. I knew that God had our paths cross because the Holy Spirit was present. My new friend and I shared many testimonies during our talk, and afterward, she invited me up to her room to talk tomorrow. The Lord knew I needed someone to talk to.

Later that day, I had a conversation with my friend about my dream concerning my grandchild. He appeared to be annoyed about something before the conversation. I stated that I wasn't sure about what God wanted me to do about the situation. He became so stern in his response. He said, "If he tells you, are you going to do it?" I looked at him puzzled, and he repeated it, louder.

I said, "Well, yes, of course." He said, "He gave you the answer now. What are you going to do about it? God doesn't hold your hand and treat you like a child. He expects things to get done, etc."

His reaction and response was shocking to me. I was left feeling as if God was telling him that I wasn't acting fast enough. That made me feel sad and confused because I know God knew I was trying. The Holy Spirit came upon me as I was holding my phone in my hand to make the phone call. I stated to him that I had my phone in my hand to call her. Well, I was going to text her first to see if she could talk right now. He waved his hand and said, "I don't care about that. It's over. God wants reaction." That hurt and bothered me at the same time.

I was left questioning why the Holy Spirit would have him talk to me this way when God knew that I analyze every reaction concerning others before I approach. He left for the weekend after that, and I was glad to not have to be around him. I lay in bed and cried, feeling as if I had let God down.

The Holy Spirit had this matter on my heart. I texted her mom to see if she could talk, and she responded yes, so I called her. She thanked me for my concern and said she understood. I was quite surprised at how well she accepted my kindness and relieved as well. I knew God was all over that conversation. God was using me to reach out to others, and I prayed that my response wasn't too late, nor that I acted out of disobedience. I'm really trying to learn the ways of the Lord, discern his voice, and act when he calls me to act, for being pleasing in his sight is what I'm aiming for.

June 5, 2018

I knew that I had to talk to her, and if I hadn't received her offer, I would regret it for the rest of my life. We sat and talked for I believe two hours and both would get emotional just talking about God's goodness. I gave her a warm embrace, and she said that she hoped that we could stay in touch. I told her definitely because God made this happen. I also told her that I wanted to send her one of my paintings as she was already thankful that I emailed her a ten-day body cleansing book because she was talking about losing weight. So we blessed each other that day.

I was so overjoyed when I left her room. I thanked God over and over. His presence was still upon me when I got home. I sat on my bed with my legs crossed, smiling and full of joy. As I began to pray, a feeling came over me. I went from praying and thanking the Lord with excitement to wailing and crying as I thanked my God for connecting me with my new friend. I felt as if God was holding me in his arms; a coolness washed over me. The feeling was so refreshing as if water was pouring over my face. I know God is cleansing me, renewing and strengthening my faith so that he can use me for great things.

God Will Speak for You

June 5, 2018

All weekend, I pondered and prayed on how I would address this issue with my friend, and God said, "He is well seasoned but not well rounded." Yes, that made sense, and I smiled. Well, Sunday, when he came home, I was ready. My thoughts were in order, the Spirit was with me, and my courage was up. Yes! He came in happy to see Maxie and me, but nope, I was ready to talk. Let me first say that he is very strong in knowledge and faith, not to mention stubborn, and believes that he is right when it pertains to the Word. I might not study as much as him, nor had I gone to a two-year Bible school, but my knowledge of the Word isn't that far distant as he makes it. He even once called me a baby Christian.

He began to tell me about his day and said that he spoke to me wrongly. He said, "I should not have said that like that." I nodded my head in agreement and said yes because I didn't like that conversation at all. He then stopped me and said that I needed to realize when a man of the spirit is apologizing. He said that God told him that he was acting as if he was him and not as the messenger. "That left me feeling as if I wasn't reacting in a timely manner. His work is done in steps. So I'm apologizing for the way I spoke to you." And he went on to say how passionate he is about getting God's work done. He was upset that my response didn't seem urgent.

My face lit up, and I began to smile as I lifted my finger to heaven and said, "Thank you, Lord." I recalled the verse for Friday, Exodus 14:14 (KJV), "The Lord shall fight for you, and ye shall hold your peace." My God, my God, you are so amazing. God had once again prepared me for this fight beforehand, and though I was recalling that scripture throughout the weekend, I didn't put it to pertain to this issue at hand.

When I learn to put this puzzle together, I'm going to be one of the best chosen vessels that God has among his people. The Lord is preparing me so well that I'm amazed. I accepted his apology with a fist bump. I wasn't feeling a hug. I was feeling like, *Nah, nah, my Father beat you up*. I wanted to tell him about this young man that I had met that worked at my job, and as usual, he took over the conversation. He takes over the conversations even when I start it.

Not My Burden to Carry

June 8, 2018

That night I slept roughly, although songs of praise were in my head when my sleep got interrupted. I felt groggy and frustrated. I couldn't remember any of my dreams, and when the alarm clock went off, I pushed the snooze twice before I got up to start my day. The spirit was on me because once again, I allowed him to overpower me with his speech, and I didn't get the chance to finish a previous conversation we had.

When I got to work this morning, my phone rang, and I was asking myself who could be calling me at 6:30 a.m., and it was the mother of the young lady that died in the car accident with my son. We spoke with each other at least once per month. God bless her beautiful soul. I told her that I was at work and couldn't talk at the moment. She was speaking with desperation and asked me to please call her back.

I go into the ladies' room at work and called her. She began to tell me that detectives had come to her house wanting to press charges against Carlos for her daughter's death. She wanted to reassure me that it was not her doing, and she didn't want Carlos, nor his family to go through anything else. She asked me to keep him in a coma, because as long as he was in a coma, they couldn't do anything to him. I told her

86

that it was all up to God and not me. She was not listening, and she was crying and reassuring me that she didn't want him to get into any trouble. After a few attempts to tell her that it was up to God, I finally just said, "Okay, I appreciate your concern." After about ten minutes. we ended the conversation.

After I hung up, I prayed for her and myself. My heart was getting heavy, and I teared up. Then God said, "Why is your heart so feeble? This is not your fight or battle. I have this. You need to focus on the journey that I have for you." With that being said, I pulled myself together and proceeded with my day.

Progress

June 12, 2018

Well, my Los Man is still here with us. God continued to heal his body. A lot had been happening over the past few months. Carlos had been pretty quiet, not much response on demand. Carlos had spent two weeks in Fairview Hospital due to an infection, but he was recovering well.

On June 10, 2018, my auntie Cindy and I were visiting, and Cindy noticed him staring at her. I got up and walked toward him, and after a few blinks, he looked at me as well. I was so happy. I then asked him to reach for my hand, and he tried to reach for my hand. I was so excited that I got weak at the knees, and I almost choked on what I was eating. I then asked him to reach for my hand a few more times as I recorded it. God was surely working in his favor.

I could tell Carlos was feeling much better since the infection was going away. He also received three units of blood due to the infection, and they believed he might be anemic as well. He was going through so much. I just cried for him, and as a mom watching her child go through this, it was so painful. My heart stayed so heavy with sorrow for him. I hadn't been happy since the accident. I felt as if I lost my joy, and I was just going through the motions day to day.

Today when I came into his room, he had vomited out of his mouth and trachea. The nurse got him cleaned up promptly. I was glad I came in when I did, although the nurse had his supplies setup to change him. She said that she had just left the room. It's okay. I was not too upset about it, but it did add to my sadness for him because all he could do was lay there and wait for someone to come. My eyes teared up; my God, the ache in my heart. I kept forgetting to say my prayer before I entered his room, "May your spirit go before me, Lord, and your glory guard me from the rear."

Carlos also had been changed to a different hallway. His room number was 102, which is closer to the nurses' station, and they could keep a better eye on him because of his falls. His dad and I worried about the changes in nurses and rooms due to his high risk of infection. He hadn't fallen out of the bed since his room change. I'd taken him outside a couple of times to get some air. The sun was a bit too bright for him. I needed to get him some sunglasses.

I was sitting here writing and watching TV when I looked to my right and noticed Carlos looking at me, eyes wide. I got up to talk to him, and he seemed to have left me again, eyes still open, just not focused on me. Well, the aides just cleaned him up, so I would put some gospel music on and take a nap before I leave, for I had to be at work at 5:30 p.m. this evening.

Deception Lurks

June 14, 2018

I had a dream a couple of days ago about my friend. In the dream, I walked in on him with another woman. I didn't recall what they were doing. I just remember that I didn't agree with the situation. I believe God was telling me that he was torn between two women. He had been spending quite a few days away from my home this week. Clarity would soon follow, so I'd just wait.

I had a dream of a large cluster of clouds with lightning going through them; no thunder or noise, just lots of lightning bolts, and the moon was beneath it and the sky was blue. It appeared to be evening time. I took this dream to mean a storm was coming for someone, or someone was going through a storm. So I said a prayer for myself and people in general. I was paying more attention to my dreams each day as well as look forward to going to bed so that I could dream. This journey was so interesting, and I just desired more and more.

Today I watched two movies, the *Son of God* and *The Gospel According to John*. Both were very close to the biblical versions. Oh, and I listened to the entire Bible on my phone and iPad, watching movies and studying. I felt that I could remember better.

The next day when I got home from work, I opened the door, and Maxie ran past me and down the stairs to the bottom down. Yes, she had done it again. This time I kept my cool, for God had told me the day before that it was the devil. So, I walked away into the kitchen as I thought, *You know what, devil, I'm not going to let you win. You want me to lose control and get out of my hookup. No, I'm not going to let you win. This is not Maxie, so you may as well get that evil spirit out of my dog.* I kept my control, stayed calm, and realized what was happening. The closer I get to God, the more Satan messes with me.

I'm so glad that God has put Holy Spirit in me to recognize Satan and his antics. God gives me wisdom and strength to fight Satan back. I am chosen by God, and He shall fight my battles as I desire to be in his presence, at all times.

I had been watching more biblical movies too. I watched *The Book of Ruth* and *Esther*. I listened to my audio Bible of Ruth, and the movie was much more detailed than the Bible, yet the same message. I had read the book of Ruth before, but a little refresher wouldn't hurt. I listened to the book of Esther again as well so as to compare it to the movie.

The Anointing

June 25, 2018

Today when I got home from work, I took a nap. I was having such a beautiful dream. I was happy. Carlos and I were together. I think we were at a hotel; I'm not sure. The room looked like a seating or dining area. Carlos was walking and talking. He was so happy and excited. OMG, I just felt the Holy Spirit hit me in my heart. As I was writing, my eyes were tearing up, and I was nervous. I looked up and asked God, "What does this feeling mean? What's going on? Come on, God, don't leave me wondering like this." At this moment, I was too scared to know the answer or admit the answer. My heart was beating faster. "Oh, Lord, my God, I ask, what's this?" I was just suddenly overwhelmed as I sat here writing and thinking of my Los Man. The voice said, "I'm giving you time." Was this my voice or God's? There were times when I had trouble discerning God's voice. I thought that in some cases, I was afraid to be right about what I heard due to the question or circumstance at the time. Right now I just told myself, *If I have the power to see things before they happen, this strongly, I don't want it. Oh, Lord, I don't know if I can be that strong. The thought of losing Carlos is weighing way too heavy on my heart at this moment. Lord, please help me to understand this feeling that I'm having right now. Please, I beg of thee, please give me clarity on this matter. Help my unbelief, Lord, my God.*

Whew, that was heavy. Okay, back to the dream. Carlos and I were talking, and I asked him how did he just get up and start walking. He said, "Well, I wobbled a little, then I just started walking." He didn't have a scar from the trachea on his neck. I asked him if he remembered anything, and he said "It was just long." I didn't understand what he meant. We were about to take a selfie when Maxie woke me up with her heavy panting. I was upset, but I got up and took her for a walk.

Lord, I need clarity and strength right now. I had to go to work. As I was walking Maxie, I was talking to God and asking what's going on. I was crying and nervous, too afraid to admit what's in my heart. I thanked God for the time he gave me Carlos and reminded myself out loud that we are not our own, and I recalled how I had given Carlos back to God, and he could do as he pleased. I only asked that God doesn't leave me to do this alone. I knew he wouldn't, but I had to say that.

Well, I didn't make it to work. I couldn't get myself together. The heaviness in my chest was still there. I was on my way to work, but I had to turn around. I was crying uncontrollably; this was heavy. *God, I don't know for sure what's going on, but my mind is racing, and I'm in a state of panic.* It's something that's not normal for me.

Oh, Lord, I need an answer, please. Clarify for me, please! Oh, it had been over two hours, and my mind and heart are still heavy. *Lord, what's going on?* This did not feel like me. I called the nursing home, and the nurse asked me if I wanted to speak to Carlos. I said yes. She put the phone to his ear, and I told him I was thinking about him and I love him.

My daughter was at her new home cleaning. I wanted to go to her to help, but I didn't want to burden her. She was trying to get her place together; she just moved in today. I was fighting the thought of Carlos dying. I was only hoping that I was wrong about my dream. I felt like

Jeremiah, Joseph, and Daniel. God spoke to me in my dreams and with visions; all of them heard God's voice through discernment, dreams, and visions. Jeremiah ran, which was how I felt right now. Joseph had to tell of bad times, which concerned Carlos right now, and Daniel predicted times to come from dreams. I also felt that. *Lord, clarify my dream, please.* I felt as if I was losing my mind. I didn't want to teach of losing a child through experience, but the Lord's will is his own; what could I do about it?

June 27, 2018

God's voice spoke to me. He said that Carlos would be made brand-new. As I walked my dog, I said to my Lord, *Your will is your will. If you are having me prepare his soul for his deliverance to you, then so be it,* for God's will is his own, and knowing that Carlos would make it to heaven is a great joy. So with that, my mind was at ease. I asked the Lord to use me in any way he wanted, so I couldn't turn back now. I did know that God would send the Holy Spirit to be with me every step of the way. Though as I wrote this, my eyes were tearing up, and the song "I'll Just Say Yes" by Brian C. Wilson was playing on my iPad. Amazing how things played out just in and on time. The way God sent healing and comfort to me right on time was so amazing.

Oh, now back to the clarity of my dream about Carlos. Later that night, or the next night I believe, it was after he told me that Carlos would be made brand-new. I dreamed that I was around some sick and ailing people, young and old. It seemed as if I was in a hospital. As I was asleep, I could feel God's presence over me. It was the same feeling I had the day before but not as strong, but I was aware of it. In the dream, I was touching and blessing the people. God said to me some would be healed and others comforted. The feeling was so very powerful. God has me on a journey that truly had me feeling as if I was immortal, like I had a superpower that wanted to be unleashed but couldn't due to my insecurities. I knew God was going to keep pushing me until I was ready to unleash to the world.

July 1, 2018

Well, I made it through today's work shift. It was a bit hectic, but I made it. Yesterday, I went to the Word Church for the 10:30 a.m. service. I knew that I needed to go. I battled with needing to talk to someone about my spiritual encounters and feelings. I needed to know if there was someone that was feeling and experiencing what I was going through.

As I was listening to the choir sing, I sang along. Holy Spirit came over me and told me that I needed to talk to someone here at the church. The desire was strong, so I knew it was God. As I was sitting, tears rolled down my face, and I said, "Okay, I will talk to someone as long as they don't give me the runaround because I know that I will lose the courage and talk myself out of it." The longer I stayed, I knew that I couldn't leave without talking to someone. God said to ask for an elder of the church. So I agreed and kept reminding myself that I had to do this. I just knew God wasn't going to let me leave regardless.

After the service, I waited for the building to clear out. I went to the Ask Me desk and told the lady there that I needed to speak to an elder. She was so kind and said, "Sure, give me a minute and let me see who's available." She returned after about 1–2 minutes and said the elder was talking, but she would let him know that I was waiting to talk with him. I was thinking that I should have asked for a lady, but maybe he was the first one she'd seen. So I dismissed the thought.

The lady at the counter went to check on his status again after about five minutes and came back to tell me that he was with a group of people, and they were talking to the pastor. After maybe five more minutes, a man approached me, asking if I was waiting for the elder. I said yes, and he said "okay, he is still in the meeting," but he would be with me. After maybe five more minutes, the lady reassured me that he would be with me and not to leave. I was nervous and holding back tears until now. The two were so kind and helpful and reassuring to me, and that eased my nerves. I asked the lady for directions to the restroom. She pointed up the stairs as she said, "Don't worry. I won't let him leave. I'll hold your spot for you."

I thanked her and hurried to the restroom so that he wouldn't be waiting on me.

When I came back, the man met me again and said the elder was finishing up and would be out. I said, "Okay, thank you." The elder approached me about 5–10 minutes later. He asked if I was looking to speak with an elder, and I said yes. He shook my hand and stated his name. I asked if we could go somewhere else to talk because I didn't want to stand here in the lobby. He said sure, so we went into the gym.

He asked, "What can I do for you?" At first, my words wouldn't come out, so I took a deep breath and said, "Okay, how can I start? Please don't think I'm crazy or anything. I'm perfectly fine." His face had a look of concern, but it didn't seem genuine. So I began to tell him that God had been speaking to me and about the dreams and visions that I'd been having. As I kept looking at him, I saw he didn't really believe me. I paused and looked up and said, "Okay, God, you told me to come and talk to him, now help me with my words."

Slowly he began to change his facial expression. He asked me to stop and said, "Okay, now what exactly is God saying to you?"

I began again, and I told him that God said my obedience was Carlos's recovery. I had seen his face and demeanor change, and I thought, *Okay, now we can talk*. I told him about my painting. I was crying through the entire conversation. I was shaking and clasping my hands while stating to him that I needed someone who believed me, who saw what I was seeing. I told him that I was not crazy; nothing was wrong with me. I knew what I was saying. I needed help figuring this all out. "Please, I need you to believe me." I told him that it was the last dream or trance that I had that really got me.

First, I started by telling him of the feeling I received. His face got more serious. I could tell that he knew that I was telling the truth, as he became more concerned. I said it hit me as I was writing about Carlos. And he said, "You had an unction." I said, "A what?" And he said "unction" as if I knew what that was.

The elder then told me that his wife deals with dreams and visions and told me to write down my name and number so that he could give it to her. I asked him if he ever had an unction, and he said yes as he nodded. He told me not to let anyone tell me or make me think that I was crazy and not to let them push me away, just to wait on his wife's phone call. He also said that the church has members that go out to visit the sick at hospitals. I said, "Yes, that's where I was. God said some will be healed, and some will be comforted." That was it; my heart felt so lifted, and I brightened up with such relief. I thanked God for pointing me to someone that understood me. I looked forward to meeting his wife.

The elder told me to go home and ask God what my purpose was for clarity because God isn't the author of confusion. I said okay, although I had my answer from my dream. After I wrote down my name, he addressed me as Sister D. Now I knew he believed me. I told him that I wasn't turning back because I had no choice.

"My son's life was on the line, so don't worry. Nothing can turn me away." Thank you, Lord. Praise God! I left and sat in the church parking lot to look up the word unction on my phone.

Unction (uhngk-shuhn) noun

1. An act of anointing, especially as a medical treatment or religious rite.

2. An unguent or ointment; salve.

3. Something soothing or comforting.

4. An excessive, affected, sometimes cloying earnestness or fervor in manner, especially in speaking.

5. Religion.

   A. The oil used in religious rights, as in anointing the sick or dying.

   B. The shedding of a divine or spiritual influence upon a person.

   C. Influence shed.

   D. Extreme unction.

6. The manifestation of spiritual or religious inspiration.

(Per Dictionary.com)

Once I read the definitions, my eyes lit up, and my heart leaped. I said, "Really, God? Me? You would give this to me?" The excitement was so unbelievable. I just couldn't fathom the thought that God felt that I was worthy enough to give me such a gift. I would never have thought that little ole me would be this blessed. I didn't know how to act, nor respond to such great news.

When I got home and told my friend about my meeting, he was glad that I reached out to someone, and he asked me why hadn't I told him about the feeling because he could have told me. He also said that all I had to do was tell the elder who he was, and he would have told me to talk to him. I didn't believe that because I felt as if he wanted to show more that he knew and wanted me to rely on him more. I had been feeling different about him. He told me he was a jealous spirit once, and I kept that in the back of my mind. I told him I was already at church when God told me to speak to him.

As I was walking my dog Maxie, I began to pray, thank, and praise God. I asked him if blessing people was what he called me to do, and he said yes. I told God that I was going to be great at it, and I wanted to please him. I promised not to let him down. I would cherish my gift and do right by it so that he wouldn't have reason to take it back from me. I so wanted to be great for my Lord God. My heart was so sincere as I held back, or at least tried to hold back, my joyful tears. God had me repeat some words after him. I couldn't remember what they were, so I supposed it was just between the two of us, but I knew it was a promise to be kept.

I called my daughter to tell her the good news, and she was so happy for me. She said, "You received your anointing," and began to cry. She said she prayed that I would find my purpose, but never did she imagine that. This was all so surreal. I also shared with two of my aunts and my mom, and they were all so happy for me. One of my aunts cried and promised to listen to God more. My sister cried as well with joy. I wanted to share with another one of my aunts, but when I went to call her, it went to voice mail. She called me back in a few minutes, and when I went to pick up the phone, it felt as if something jolted my hand and made me drop it. I felt nervous, so I put the phone back down as I peeked to see who it was. I felt as if the Holy Spirit didn't want me to tell her, so I said, "Okay, Lord, I won't tell her." It puzzled me for days. I'd let God handle that.

I knew that God was doing something in my life, but never ever did I feel that I was this worthy. I was still in awe, but I had to let this sink in and put on my best to make my Lord proud of me. I would cherish this precious gift. I felt like a superhero, full of power, but didn't know how to use it, nor release it. But I would be an A-plus servant as I learned. I didn't know how long it would take, but I did know that "patience is a virtue," and patience I had. I couldn't wait to learn how to use my gift, no matter how long it took or how hard the journey. Darnice Renee Harrison is all in! You can count on me, Jesus! I was beginning to realize that my dreams were telling me that Carlos was about to face a trial and would triumph. So when I would have troubling dreams and in the end, I would be holding him, I knew he would recover from his illness.

My Eyes Are Opening

July 5, 2018

I watched the *Gospel of Paul* and learned a lot about him. Even though I read about him in the Bible, watching the movie seemed to give me more understanding. I recalled a lot of the events from the Bible and my daily readings. I also finished the book *Final Quest* by Rick Joyner. It seemed I was reading all that I needed at the exact time that God needed me to.

I learned that there are different levels of heaven. There's a high level and a lower level, but you are still in heaven. My goal is to be in the higher level and sit next to those that followed God and lead the people to seek him and not the one delivering the message. I want to always look to Jesus and God for my daily anointing and not to myself. Some that are in heaven's lower level are there because they forgot where the power and word was coming from. So since God had promised them that they would go to heaven, he kept his promise although they fell short of his glory. I pray that I always remember to pay respect to Jesus and my Lord God. I really want to show my utmost appreciation for the gift that He has given me. I only pray that I am able to handle the job on my heart, for I will be expected to share more love than I can imagine to friends, family, and strangers. I pray for the removal of judgement from my mind and heart so that it is filled with love and compassion. God keeps his promises. How much honor you give depends on how high of a seat you will occupy in heaven; it all depends on you. I had shared my anointing with my family because I want my family to make it to heaven so that we could be together in eternity. I prayed for them and with them. I pray that they take heed to all I had said and learn to get to know God wholeheartedly.

I praise God daily and, after, cry my eyes out, sometimes until my head hurt. I'm so full of anxiousness and thankfulness. I just thank God daily, multiple times a day. To be someone that was made to feel so unworthy, used, a thief, whorish, and ugly by family and others, it was hard for me to believe that God sees me so worthy of such a precious gift. I knew that I was missing something, and I yearned for more, I didn't know, nor expect that God had a gift waiting just for me.

I had a dream that I was driving down the street, and I stopped to pick up a boy around the age of 7–9 years of age. I drove him to the grocery store, and as I sat in the parking lot, I was holding a toddler in my lap. We were pretending that he was driving as I was bouncing him on my lap, just having fun. I don't remember where the toddler came from. After a while, I felt as if the little boy was taking longer in the store than I expected. So I decided to go in. I asked the toddler if he wanted something out of the store as I picked him up. He was so excited. As I walked around the store, I was looking at various snacks as the toddler followed close behind me. I stopped to look at some popsicles as I asked the toddler if he wanted some. I got no response, so I looked down, and he was not there.

His name came to me as Carlos, so I started calling out Carlos so that he could hear and answer me. I began to get frantic as I got no response. I saw another boy on his phone, and it was my son Chuck. I yelled to him, "Where's Carlos? You were supposed to be watching him." How he came about I don't know, but he shrugged his shoulders and remained on the phone.

I continued searching for Carlos, and I passed by two ladies. One was holding a child in her arms. He had straight shoulder-length hair, so I knew that wasn't Carlos. I asked them if they had seen a small boy walking around, as I overheard them say, "I hope he finds his mom." The ladies pointed to a door and said, "Someone took him back there." I went to the door and called for Carlos. He came out from behind the door alone. His eyes were bloodshot and open wide as if he'd been frightened. I was thinking of how scared he must be, so I didn't yell at him for walking away. I picked him up and hugged him tightly, and the dream ended.

The Connection of the Dream

July 12, 2018

This morning I received a phone call from the nursing home. The nurse told me that Carlos was running a fever and was breathing a little unsteady. She said that they called his doctor and would give him some Tylenol and monitor him. There's no need for him to go to the hospital. I thanked her and hung up. After the phone call, I got my Bible to read and study some verses. I got up to check my phone, and I saw a missed call from the nursing home. It was at 9:18 a.m. when the call was made. They left a voice mail. I looked at my phone in confusion for it was now after 10:15 a.m. The message said that Carlos was having trouble breathing and that he needed to be taken to the hospital. His fever had risen, and his blood pressure was dropping. They were calling the ER. Her voice sounded panicked. Holy Spirit came over me as I was on the phone. I felt the need to get to Carlos, but I thought about working out first, because that was a part of my plans for the day before my visit to Carlos. I had seen a text from his dad saying that he had received a message from the nursing home, and he wanted to ride with me.

As Holy Spirit urged me to get to Carlos, I said, "Sure, I'll pick you up, and I will be there around 11:00 a.m. He said, "Okay."

I picked up my Bible and asked the Lord to please give me a word to hold on to. Holy Spirit was urging me to get to Carlos now, so I put off working out and began flipping through the pages of my Bible while asking God to give me a word. I was a little frantic but not nervous. I knew God was with me because I could feel his presence. I first turned to Hebrews 8, skimmed through it, and said "no, that's not it." I told myself to just listen. I repeated it over and over. I urged God for a word. I was soon led to Matthew 8, and I knew I heard it well. I felt better as the Holy Spirit was constantly telling me to get to Carlos.

I left to pick up his dad, and we headed to the hospital. The devil tested me on my drive to see Carlos. As we were driving on the highway, a white van carrying a ladder and supplies on top of it forced me out of my lane so that he could get in front of me. I kept my cool. I just said, "Really, truck, seriously," with my hand up and my face in disbelief. His dad said, "Look at this man. Watch it."

I kept calm, for my mind was totally on Carlos, and the Holy Spirit was constantly telling me to get to Carlos. I moved over to the lane on my left, sped up, and got in front of the van. After about two minutes, his dad was looking out of the window, and he pointed out a red van. He said that he was thinking that if he was driving the red van, and the white van had done that to him, he would've clipped the white van so that he could spin out. I knew that the enemy was trying to distract me.

I calmly said, "Why? So that he could cause a chain reaction for the cars behind him, and others get hurt? That's not right." Then he said that he deserved it.

I said, "No, that wouldn't do anything but hurt innocent people, and the guy in the white van would end up surviving, while someone else dies." He says the guy was very wrong for cutting me off. I said, "Yes, he was very much so wrong, but I will let God handle him. No one got hurt. We are fine, and it's okay. No need in fighting wrong with wrong."

Once we arrived at the ICU, we were told that Carlos had just arrived at the unit and was being assessed. I wondered why it took so long because at least three hours had passed since the phone call. We had to wait in the sitting area for about an hour or so. The nurse then came out to let us know that it was okay to go in and see Carlos. He was in room 32. When we walked in his room, there were two nurses tending to him. Carlos was looking so scared. He was choking and coughing. His face was red, his lips twisted as he strained and gasped for air. His eyes were bloodshot and bulging out. He looked like he did in my dream, eyes bloodshot and face scared.

We were told that he had to be resuscitated three or four times, and it took six nurses and doctors to work on him because his trachea was blocked and that we should report the nursing home for neglect. I was stunned, but I was glad that we didn't lose him, and God allowed us to have one more day together. I tried not to think about the neglect because my mind didn't have the strength to concentrate on lawsuits.

For a brief moment, I started to panic, then I looked at his dad and saw the scared look on his face as he leaned forward and said "Carlos—" I said, "No, don't. I got it, I got it." Holy Spirit was telling me to touch him and pray. I asked why was his face so swollen, and the nurse said it was due to the fluids that he had been given. I asked Holy Spirit what I should do. He replied, *Touch him and pray.*

I said, *Okay, I'll wait until the nurses leave.* He said to touch him and pray over and over again. So I washed my hands and went over to his bed.

I put one hand on Carlos's chest and one hand on his head. I closed my eyes and began to pray as fast as I'd ever prayed before. His dad was on the other side of the bed, reassuring him that he was going to be okay. I prayed over him for about 2–3 minutes, and then I sat down and continued to pray as I rocked back and forth. The nurse was giving him Tylenol and antibiotics. After thirty minutes, Carlos's breathing went from 91 to 51. Praise God! The swelling in his face was going down, and his eyes were no longer bulging. His dad said that he was looking better, and the nurses said that he was improving and the Tylenol was working fast as well. I said yes, he should be. I told his dad to stick around me, and he'd get used to it because I was getting used to it. I was speaking of the power of prayer. Praise God!

The nurses were talking to each other, and one said to the other to work her magic and find a vein to stick him in. I said, "We will leave the magic to the devil and his people. Right now we have faith and prayer in this room." The nurse stated that it was just a figure of speech, and she had strong belief in God. I said, "It's okay, but we are working with faith and prayer only." I looked to his dad. "If they think Tylenol worked this fast, they've got to be kidding. Ain't no Tylenol ever worked this fast." We stayed with Carlos for over two hours, and he was good and stable when we left.

After our visit, I explained to Carlos's dad how God wanted us to stop with the evil thoughts and words. If we love God and say we believe in him and listen to him, we have to change our way of thinking. He agreed with me and nodded his head.

Doubt

July 15, 2018

I went to visit my Los Man, and when I looked at him, he looked like someone had punched him in both of his eyes. When he opened his eyes, they were red, very red, and his right eye had a broken vessel in the corner; you could barely see any white in his eyes. The nurse said he had an eye infection. This disturbed me. The more I looked at him, the sadder I felt. The nurse also said that they believe at one point, Carlos went into septic shock. Some improvement was happening as far as his blood pressure and kidney, but one lung had gotten worse, but it was okay.

My sister was with me. Both of us took turns praying for him. I played some music as tears rolled down my face. My sister pulled up a powerful prayer from her phone. I read it to him. I also read from Matthew 8:12–16 or so. Sometimes I just couldn't help but cry. My faith wasn't shaken or anything; I just felt for my son so deeply when I saw him hurting. He coughed really hard a few times and turned red all over from the strain. It looked like he was struggling to get it out. I prayed for my son and family, and then we left. Tonight I prayed so hard for my family that I cried. I just want my entire family with me in heaven. I know it is way beyond peaceful and beautiful.

July 16, 2018

Today I woke up with Carlos on my mind. I felt sad for him. The infection in his eyes looked painful. When he coughed, he turned so red from the struggle. His tongue had a thick white film on it because he couldn't open his mouth long enough to get his teeth brushed. He only opened it to yawn. Although I knew God was taking care of Carlos, as his mother, the pain still hit me hard at times. I'd gotten much better at handling what he was going through, but it was still very tough.

As I walked Maxie this morning, I asked God for strength to continue on. I asked for forgiveness if I was being doubtful of his promise and to please understand that I feel for my son. I knew that this was all to strengthen me for what was to come, for if I couldn't handle what Carlos was going through, how could I handle what I was going to come in contact with, the illness of those God would send me to heal and bless? I felt as if Carlos was my first patient, so to speak, and if I could pass this test, which was the hardest because he is my flesh and blood, then I shall be able to pass many, many more.

July 17, 2018

Today, the social worker for Fairview Hospital called and said that Carlos's doctor suggested that he be moved to a more skilled facility because he was on a ventilator for a while, and the Normandy didn't have the technology to handle him right now. Carlos's eyes were not infected; they were red due to straining and pressure from coughing. I kept picturing how scared he was when he went to the hospital. The fact that he couldn't breathe had to be terrifying for him.

The pneumonia was worse today than yesterday. The doctor believed it was due to him maybe lying on one side of his body. His kidneys were improving, and blood pressure was good. He went into septic shock. That was the reason for the added complications besides the pneumonia. But he was better despite it all. I asked Carlos if I could hold his hand, and he reached for me immediately. That really made his dad and I smile. He also gave his dad a moment of good eye contact which excited his dad.

I prayed so hard to God today before I went to see my Los Man. God didn't seem to be answering me. I turned to the back of my Bible and looked up verses on praying. I read Luke 11:1–13, John 14:12–14, James 5:13–16, and 1 John 5:14–15. I prayed these verses over and over and spoke to God, telling him his words and his promises back to him. But God wouldn't respond back. I didn't know if I was too anxious right now or if God was testing my faith and patience.

All I knew was that I was not going to lose my faith in God, nor prayer. I was sad, and I cried hard as I prayed today. I felt as if my life was at a standstill. I was trying not to worry about my groceries, finances, or bills. My relationship with my friend was on hold because I really didn't know who or if God had a mate for me. I felt so alone right now. I really needed God to answer my questions. He did send Holy Spirit for strength when I asked today, so I did thank him for that.

Although I was a little distant from my friend and Carlos's dad—well, from everybody—I did feel better since leaving Carlos today. My friend asked me what was going on with me because I hadn't spoken much lately. I told him that I didn't want to talk right now. He said, "Obviously." But he didn't push me. I appreciated that. I had been thinking about what to say to him all the ride home, which was a fifteen-to-twenty-minute ride. I stared out the window and looked to the sky to see if God was going to give me a sign of some sort. But he didn't. I'd just keep waiting. My dreams hadn't made much sense to me lately either. I dreamed but don't really remember them.

Perhaps God would talk to me tonight. I miss his voice. I prayed that he wasn't talking to me, and I was not discerning his voice. *Lord, I feel lost without you. Where are you? Talk to me, Lord. I've cried out to you, and you don't answer, yet my faith still remains.*

My sister suggested that we do Bible study together. I think I'd take her up on that offer. I felt some type of way toward some of my family members because they failed to inquire about Carlos's well-being. When I post an update on FB, they were quick to say amen or "I'm praying for you," but they didn't call, text, or visit. I kept saying it's a good thing that I have God, which is awesome, but I did wish my family was more involved, at least his brothers, aunts, uncles, and cousins that he grew up with. We have a very large family.

My aunt would have a birthday card party. I wondered how many family members would show up for that. At this moment, I doubt very seriously that I would attend. I love them all, but I felt as if so many of them were way too fake for my spirit right now. Well, it's late, so I would read my Bible before bed.

Troubled Dream

July 18, 2018

I slept pretty hard last night; can't quite remember my dream or dreams. I woke up a few times during the night because of noise. I looked at the clock at one point. It was after midnight, then again it was after 2:00 a.m. The alarm woke me up at 4:30 a.m. which startled me, and my body felt as if I had a hangover. That wasn't true because I didn't have any alcohol to drink.

Maxie woke me up when she opened the bedroom door around 6:00 a.m. After falling back asleep, I had this dream. I was lying on my back because I remember tossing for a better position. In my dream, I was in a new home with a man. He had to be my mate because I was sitting on the porch, and he was sitting next to me caressing me. My brother was there. He was wiping down the lounge chair, and it was going from dull to shiny. It was one of those older chairs made of plastic strips of yellow, green, and white. I remember those from my childhood. I was amazed at how the dullness was being removed because they didn't appear to be dirty.

I then noticed a car pull up on the porch next to us. It looked to have come right through the porch door. I pointed it out to the guy I was with, and my brother said, "That's how the garages are here. The driveway comes all the way up." I thought that was strange because we were upstairs on a porch. I looked around and noticed all the houses were on a hill, but from the front of the house, you didn't know that the houses were on a hill.

So the car actually came from the side of the house, because I could see the asphalt driveway and a parked car in the neighbor's yard. My brother began to tell us about a scheme that pays for college. I asked him what he was talking about. He went on to say, "I tried to tell you two about it before." I said that I didn't remember, so he went on to tell me about it, and I said that I didn't want anything to do with it. I didn't want to get caught up in any mess.

Water began to come up onto the porch as if someone was using a hose to spray up from the ground. The person downstairs was washing his porch, but my porch was getting wet. At first I thought I wanted my friend to tell them that my porch was getting wet, but then I thought, well, there's nothing over there getting wet, so I didn't care. I went back to thinking about the chairs and said we were going to have to clean all the chairs now.

My friend was caressing me in front of my brother. He was squeezing my breast and kept putting his fingers in my mouth. I kept turning my head to keep him from putting his fingers in my mouth. My brother left, and it was just my friend and I, and he asked me if I had a broom because he couldn't find one and that I needed one. I told him that there was one downstairs. I felt myself getting nervous and uncomfortable.

My friend tried to kiss me, and I was resisting. He apologized to me for what he had done to me, not really saying what he had done, but I knew he had done something harmful because of how I felt. He laid his body on top of me and tried to kiss me again, but I kept turning my head and tried to get up or push him off of me. He grabbed a cover and put it over his head so I could barely see his face as he said, "I'm just going to lie here with you for a while." I heard myself telling myself that this was getting scary, and I needed to wake up from the dream. I could really feel myself panicking and getting nervous while I was asleep, but I was aware of what was going on.

The guy continued to force me to lie down. As he caressed me, he noticed that I was uncomfortable. He looked at me as if he couldn't believe that I was still nervous after he had apologized. It felt so real, I could feel hands on me. I woke from the dream and I was on my back with my arms up as if I was pinned down and my heart was racing. I lay like this for a few minutes asking God who was this guy in my dream because I knew that I wouldn't ever go back to my ex.

The name of the guy that the lady I met at work named came to mind, and I asked God again, *Who is this man?* and his name came to mind again. I begin to think to myself, *Does this guy have a dark side? Did God tell me no when I asked him had he sent him for me? Is this why I've been feeling uncomfortable lately because I didn't listen when God answered me?* I'm confused right now.

My brother would never get involved in a crooked scheme, and my ex was verbally and physically abusive toward me. My ex always thought that he could apologize to me because he was mad at the time. He thought that I should or would forgive him, and everything was okay soon afterward. But my pain lasted a few days after someone that said they love me hurt me. It took a while for me to get comfortable again.

So I did know that God revealed in my dream that this person was trying to put me in the same position that was not good for me. God was letting me know that this person was not good for me. Well, I asked God if he had sent this guy, and I got this dream. If this was the guy that God was revealing to me, then so be it. I also thought about my friend. I also had asked God if he was the one for me as well.

I had never seen the guy's face in my dream clearly, but I knew that he was taller than me and had a dark complexion. I would just keep waiting on God. Thank you, Lord, for speaking to me in my dreams. My friend had been asking me what I dreamed about 3–4 times a week, and so finally I told him about this dream. He asked me if I knew who it was. I looked at him strangely and said no. I was thinking to myself, *It could be you*. At this moment, I didn't trust anyone.

July 20, 2018

Carlos was improving, and I thank the Lord Jesus Christ for that. I watched the movie *I Am Gabriel* yesterday, and oh, how my heart lit up. It was such an amazing showing of God's grace, mercy, and power. The movie was awesome. I wondered and spoke to God with such joy in my heart of how he would one day use me to bless and heal others. The thought almost brought me to tears. I knew that I would have cried if I wasn't at work. The feeling that I felt to be able to one day be used by God to heal a person was absolutely joyful. My eyes and heart lit up with a happiness that I couldn't quite explain. The Lord himself anointed me. He didn't have one of his priests, pastors, servants, or any other of his called do it. He felt that I was so special to him that he did it himself. That realization really hit me this day and moment. God loves me just that much.

God Sends Clarity and Encouragement

July 25, 2018

Oh my, so much had been happening since Friday. My adrenaline had finally calmed down enough for me to write down all the events from the past few days. So let's start with Friday. My spiritual sister was in the restaurant standing in the buffet line. I smiled with amazement when I saw her. I hugged her and called her name. She smiled and said, "You know this trip was spur of the moment." I said, "Really?" She said, "Yes, it's my husband and my thirty-fifth anniversary, and he decided that we should come and spend it with some old friends of ours." I was so excited I told her how she had been on my mind. I said, "God sent you." She said, "You think so?" I said, "I know he did because I needed to talk to you. I have so much to tell you."

I told her quickly about the day Carlos went to the hospital for pneumonia. I told her how God was coming to me faster and faster and how I said "God, you usually give me two days. Now it's only a couple of hours." She laughed and said, "You just wait until he gives you no notice." My eyes got big, and I could feel Holy Spirit. I said, "Girl, I'm about to stop talking to you. You're scaring me.

She smiled and said, "You will be ready." I smiled and said, "I know."

The restaurant was busy that day, so I had to get back to work, and when I came back, she was gone. I really hate that I didn't get the chance to ask her what room she was in because I wanted to talk. I missed her so much. I was looking forward to Saturday so that I could see her again. I wrapped a painting that I did for her, and I also had a card that I made for her and her husband. I put them in a Victoria's Secret bag because that's all I had at the time.

Well, she didn't come down for breakfast, and I had been eagerly waiting to see her. I went to the restroom and sent her an email letting her know that I had a package for her. After a couple of hours and no response, I went to the front desk to get her room number. I called her and didn't get an answer. I hoped that she hadn't left and gone back home without saying goodbye.

On Sunday, I called her room, and she answered. I told her that I had a package to drop off, and she said 3:00 p.m. would be fine. I said, "Okay, I'll see you then."

When I got to her room, she invited me in. Her husband went into the other room to give us some privacy. She really loved the painting and said that they were looking to buy a new home, and she knew exactly where she was going to put it. I told her that I felt the painting was her and that she could sit back and look at it when she needed to think, and her mind could go into the forest. Actually, the painting matched the outfit she had on.

We talked for two hours, and she explained the dream of the man trying to take advantage of me. She said that the cleaning of the chairs meant that the house was getting cleaned, and someone was leaving. Water coming up and flowing back down the hill meant that the old was washing away, and the man covering up his head was deceit. It explained exactly what I was going through. My friend was distancing himself from me. I no longer had feelings for him being a mate for me.

And she said that the devil knew that he was leaving my life, and he was losing, so he tried to bring this other guy into my life as a replacement to get me off track and distracted.

I said to myself, *That was a weak try from the devil.* She said I passed that test from the devil.

She said that God told her this morning that my friend was causing confusion and contrariness in me, and I needed to get him out of my life. God wasn't going to come to me in the middle of confusion; two spirits should be on one accord. She started crying as she said I needed to get that man out of my bed so that I could heal my son. She said that Carlos and I were suffering longer than we had to. God was waiting on me, and my son might be as well. She asked me if I knew that God was waiting on me. I said that I thought that I was waiting on God.

She said, "No, God is ready. He is waiting on you." She was so stern, honest, and caring. She said that I needed to make a decision.

And I said, "Well, you don't see me taking up for him, so that's easy." She said that spirits couldn't get in him, but it could be a spirit behind all that's going on. Considering where he worked, there were all sorts of evil going on. She asked me what I was going to do again, and I said that I was going to let her know later today. I said God might have already told him. She asked me if I thought so. I said, "Yes, God always talk to him first, and I can tell by the way he had been acting lately." I had told my sister and daughter that I felt a little jealousy coming from him due to what he would say at times, like he didn't want to hear of my talking to the elders at the church and how I knew God had prepared them. He said that my anxiety level was up, so I stopped talking. I said that I couldn't believe that God felt I was worthy enough to be trusted with such a gift, and he told me I wasn't worthy. I would get sad about Carlos when he would fall ill, and he would make me feel guilty about my feelings. He would tell me that I was just a baby at this when we would read the Bible or talk deeply about spirituality. I recalled him saying to me that I better tell God how mad I was about what's going on and how he would speak to God like that. He said if God didn't speak to him, he would just not speak to God either. I was shocked at that statement, and I could never do that. I tried to express my anger to God, but I didn't feel right about doing that at all.

My spiritual sister said that my friend knew that I was more spiritually mature than him. I knew that, but I just needed more clarity. God sent her to me, and she knew it Sunday morning. It was after 6:00 p.m. when I got home Sunday. As I approached my home, my spirit was stirring, and I was feeling nervous and I didn't quite know why. I soon found out it was because my friend was there. I was supposed to pick my mom up at 5:00 p.m. to go visit Carlos, but I was running late, so I quickly changed my clothes and promised myself that I would talk to him when I got back. When I returned home, he wasn't there, and actually, I was relieved. I knew my spiritual sister was waiting on a response, but I wanted to wait until I talked to him first.

When I went to bed Sunday night, I couldn't sleep. I woke up at 11:00 p.m., then at midnight, and again after 1:00 a.m. Then Maxie barked after 2:30 a.m., so I got up to see what it was. I thought it was my friend, but it was my neighbor downstairs coming in. My spirit stirred in my stomach even more, so I said, "Okay, I know what this is. God, you are trying to talk to me, so I laid down, and go ahead, God, I'm listening." Almost immediately after I closed my eyes, I could feel the Holy Spirit come over me. I fell asleep thinking about the conversation my mom and uncle had earlier about him taking her to the credit union on Wednesday.

In my dream, I was riding in his truck, and he started driving faster and faster. I could feel my spirit spinning, and it sounded as if a fan was spinning really fast in my ears. I almost panicked, but then I heard a voice say over and over, "Just let it happen. It's okay." And I said okay, then my spirit stirred even faster, then the next thing I knew, I felt as if I was standing up in the car, and my head was through the sunroof of my uncle's truck, and it was pitch-dark. There were these chalk drawings of all kinds of animals circling around my head. I was amazed. There were birds, lions, flies, frogs, and I really remembered the elephant. As I was pointing to them and in the midst of my excitement, I heard the gentlest voice say, "Hello, Darnice." And I said with such joy as a five-year-old at a carnival on a merry-go-round, "Hi, God." I clasped my hands around my mouth and said softly, "Hi." The voice came from my left. I never saw his face, but I could feel him smiling at me with such warmth. I felt so warm and loved. He allowed me to play with the animals a little longer. They were perfect drawings as if I drew them. I felt the spinning slow down and stop, then the spirit left and let me sleep.

At 4:30 a.m. my alarm clock went off. I thought that I would be sleepy and tired before I went to sleep, but I wasn't. I felt so refreshed. I stood up, and after about five minutes or so, I thought about my night, and I said, "I remember you spoke to me, God. You spoke to me. I remember everything." I clasped my face and sat back down on the bed and marveled at the thought, then I looked into the mirror and told myself, *God loves you, Donnie*, over and over as tears ran down my face. And I said I love you too. For the first time in fifty years, I was able to really tell myself as I looked in the mirror that I loved myself truly.

I heard that same gentle voice say, "Do you want some more?" I said yes. Then he said, "Then you know what you have to do." I said yes. I felt that joy for the entire day. I smiled and felt so loved like never before. I told my mom, children, and ex-husband all in the same day with the same excitement.

On Monday, Carlos was accepted at Regency Hospital in Middleburg Heights, Ohio. I knew that he would be healed, in Jesus's name. Later on, when I was on my way home, my spirit started stirring in an uncomfortable nervous way. I said okay, either my friend was at the house, or something was going on. I got in the house, and Maxie had an accident, so I thought that was it. I went into my bedroom and saw that there was a hundred-dollar bill on my dresser, and my friend had clothes on the bed. So then I knew the feeling was because he had been there. He didn't come back, so I thought it would be a good time to paint him that picture that I promised him, and this way, there would be no reason for him to contact me after he left for good. I painted a picture of him kneeling before Jesus and a cross with a beautiful amber sunset in the background.

Well, he hadn't come back yet, and I planned to hang around the house today in case he came by. I was asked to go in to work, but I believed this talk was more important.

Last night I felt my spirit, and I had a dream about eagles. I was riding in the passenger seat with a man pulling a large vehicle. It was silver and looked like something used at carnivals and shaped like a rocket. There were different rides being pulled behind him with people on bikes. We were on a bike as well.

As he rode me through the streets, I spotted an eagle sitting in someone's yard to my left. It looked like a young eagle, for its hair was still fluffy. I was surprised to see an eagle in the city. I said to the man, "Look, is that an eagle?" He looked and said yes, not as surprised as me. We rode further, and I saw another eagle on my left in a ditch on the curb. It was sitting in a nest with 4–5 eggs in it, then there was an eagle flying up above and over the nest.

I wondered if I could fly, and the driver said, "You can." So I stood up and began to fly. I flapped my arms, and the harder I flapped, the higher I went. I was a little unsteady at first, then I got the hang of it. The man told me to be careful not to go too high; I was just a beginner. I smiled and said I got it. As I landed back on the bike—well, it was more like one of those carts with two seats in the front; I guess like a large tricycle but two seats in the front—the man caught me around my waist.

I recalled the dream, and I looked up the meaning of eagles in dreams, and here's what I got from Google: "To see an eagle in your dreams symbolizes nobility, pride, fierceness, superiority, courage, and powerful intellectual ability. It also represents self-renewal and your connection with your spirituality."

Also "they bring a sense of courage and desire to explore and grow. To dream of a flying eagle or one that is perched high signifies good fortune or victory coming your way."

I went to sleep anticipating hearing God's voice in my ear. I really love his soft and gentle tone. The thought of his voice just makes my heart and soul smile. I went to sleep wondering what I was going to dream next.

About 2:40 p.m., I was taking a nap and woke to a text from my friend—well, a voice message—asking me to open the door because he will be here in a few. My spirit went wild. That uncomfortable feeling took over me so strongly. I got weak, and my body shook as I listened to the message and headed toward the back door to let him in. The closer I got to the door, the more my spirit stirred, and my legs got weak. I had to literally hold onto the handrail as I went down the stairs. I looked as if I was crawling down the steps. I was so confused and couldn't understand why I was feeling so shaken up. I'd never felt that nervous in my life.

As I went down the stairs, I said to my spirit, *Okay, I'm going to do it.* I didn't speak to him. I went straight to my room and sat on the bed, still shaking. I was short of breath, and I kept telling myself that I had to do it. I asked God for strength to follow through. I knew that I wasn't going to be disobedient to God. I didn't like this feeling at all. I couldn't handle this uncomfortable feeling at all.

When my friend came into the house, he noticed the painting on the table. He said, "Wow, that's nice. I like that." He came into the room and handed me the mail from the mailbox, then asked me who the painting was for. I said, "It's for you."

He asked why I had painted him a painting. So I began with "God told me that I had to tell you to leave." He said, "Okay, can I ask why?" He was calm and soft-spoken. I said, "Because our spirits can't work together. He says you are causing me confusion and hindrance." He nodded and said, "Okay." "God wants me alone here because he can't work in confusion, and he's trying to set me in position to heal my son and get him out of that bed."

He agreed and asked me for a hug as he said "Hallelujah, I receive that. Glory to God." I was still sitting as he came around the bed. He paused and asked if I was allowed to hug him. I said, "Sure, just give me a chance to stand up."

My knees were still weak and shaking, my voice was trembling as I spoke.

As we hugged, he said, "Hallelujah, glory." I said, "I'm sorry, but I have to do what I have to do." I told him about my welcome dream and how God had called my name, even after he had said he wouldn't call me again.

He took a shower, and afterward, I was telling him how my spirit had gotten so much stronger. I could feel when he had been here and when he was here. As I was talking, I saw him on the opposite side of the bed with his arms stretched out wide, head bent down, and praying. I heard him sniffling, so I knew he was crying. I remained silent. He started telling me how he had slowly started packing his belongings, waiting on clarity, then he left to go into the bathroom, sobbing heavily, and he shut the door behind.

After a few minutes, he asked for a hug, and it was a tight embrace.

I told him, "I love you."

And he said, "I love you too." I told him that I appreciated all that he had done, and I wished him nothing but the best. I told him he would be okay, and he said, "I'm good." I told him that I always thank God for sending him as I teared up. I let him know that he would be the first to know when my son woke up and I would continue to watch his videos and maybe our paths would cross again one day. He said, "Yes, you prefer to speak to me online anyway."

I knew it was a little joke, but I said nothing. He hugged me continuously throughout our conversation.

He appeared to be truly happy for me. He asked if I could leave the key so that he could get his things. I said sure. He asked if he had to go today or when. I said, "I don't know when, but soon. Today, if you can." He said that he had nowhere to go, but he had been working on it. I wished him nothing but the best, and he left because he had to go volunteer somewhere; I didn't ask where. I never gave him the letter.

I prayed wholeheartedly for him and asked God if I did well. I didn't recall hearing God's response, but I knew that he was proud of me for obeying his word. I said, "God, I'm free and ready to do whatever you need me to do. No more confusion, and nothing in my way. I'm ready to heal my son."

A Healing Vision

July 27, 2018

This morning as I was driving on my way to work, I was admiring the clouds in the sky when I got a vision in my head. My children's dad and I were at the hospital with Carlos. I was praying over him, and he sat up, eyes wide open. His father began to rejoice saying, "Look, Donnie, he's awake, look." He was very overjoyed. I was praising and thanking God over and over while saying "I told you, I told you. God said he was going to do it."

The nurses and the doctors came in. I was not sure if they came because of the noise or if his dad called for them to come in. The nurses were in awe, and the doctors asked what happened. I said God did it. They checked Carlos out and couldn't find anything wrong with him. Praise God.

After the vision, as I was driving I said "I see it, God, I see it," and began crying worshipping and praising the Lord. I was so excited because I knew the Lord was telling me that Carlos's healing was on the way. I texted his dad, aunt, and siblings as well as my sister and told them about it. I later spoke to my aunt on the phone because I needed someone to talk to. She said she believed, and that made me feel good.

I kept my good mood the entire day, until around 12:30 p.m., I started to feel overwhelmed. I asked the Holy Spirit to please wait until I got off work. The prayer worked until about 1:30 p.m. I couldn't hold back any longer, so I left work. I thought that I was going to see Carlos, but I went into a crying spell and ended up at my sister-in-law's house, and we talked for a long time. It really helped.

I felt as if his dad and brother didn't believe 100 percent, and if they did, the power of prayer would be stronger. But God only needed me to believe, and he would still heal Carlos. I just got overwhelmed at any time. I couldn't control it sometimes; it's a lot to handle.

Later, Carlos's dad and I went to visit him, and he was looking very uncomfortable and had mucus all over his trachea and neck. That upset us both. He was having trouble breathing from coughing. We had the nurses change and clean him up. Carlos's eyes were looking much better. The swelling in his face had gone down, and he belched three times in a row. We laughed. That was a first for him. We left after an hour because I had to be at my second job. I was doing very well until about 8:45 p.m. The overwhelming feeling came back, and I began to cry. I hurried and finished up my work and left around 9:20 p.m. A lady noticed and asked if I was okay. I said yes, and she snuck a hug anyway, but that was okay.

I cried all the way home as I asked God why I kept feeling like this. I said, "We have the house to ourselves. I will do whatever you want me to do. I don't understand why I feel this way. You have all of me. There's no love for any other man in my life but you. I don't understand. We can talk when I get home, just grant me traveling mercy, please.

I'm free. You have all of me, Lord, all of me." Well, now I would walk Maxie, then fall asleep talking to God.

The Feeling Explained

July 29, 2018

Today was a better day than yesterday; thank God. My aunt and I visited Carlos today. He looked so much better. He had been off the ventilator for two days now and was breathing well. Praise God, our Lord Almighty.

Yesterday I was still feeling overwhelmed from the night before. I needed clarity for the way I felt when I told my friend that he had to leave. I was beginning to feel as if it just couldn't be God that was making me feel so bad, not if wanted me to speak his word and do his will. So when I got to work at 6:00 a.m., my mind was weak, and I knew that I could break down crying any moment. I told my supervisor that I was going to try to make it through the day. I sang the song "Confidence," constantly trying to strengthen myself. I asked Holy Spirit for strength as well. Finally, about 7:00 a.m., I broke. My co-worker asked me if I was okay. I said no. She said, "You are ready for your baby to be healed." I said yes. My supervisor asked me if I wanted to go home. I just walked away and headed toward the locker room with tears rolling down my face. My coworker said "Aww, Darnice" as she followed behind me. When we got into the locker room, she just held me as I cried, and she prayed and cried and prayed and cried. She held me for about fifteen minutes or more.

When I got myself together, I told her about the feeling and how bad it felt. I was shaking as I recalled the day. She was amazed and praised God as she told me that God allowed me to feel the evil spirit so that I would know what it felt like because I would be encountering it in people. So I needed to know how it felt in order to cast it out and heal people. She said that the spirit didn't want to leave and didn't want me to obey God. It knew that I was trying to figure out who I was and that God was about to use me, so it tried to block me from telling my friend to leave.

I looked up and said, "I knew God wouldn't make me feel like that. I knew it."

Her being able to clarify that for me made me feel so much better. She mumbled to herself with a smile that God had allowed her to be able to discern that for me. I began to think about the three previous times I had felt that spirit before I told my friend that he had to leave. I thanked her over and over, then I left to go home at around 7:30 a.m.

I saw another coworker, and she tried to joke with me, but she could tell that I wasn't feeling it, so she just hugged me and said, "I hope you feel better. You don't have to say anything, just give me a hug." There was another person with her, and she hoped I felt better as well.

I got to my car and just cried all the way home. I tried to call my sister but got no answer, so I decided to go to church. My sister called me around 8:30 a.m., and we talked for a while. She told me about the food bank that they were having at her church, and I told her that I would come. I picked her up from her house and dropped her off at her church to help with the distribution of the food. I left and went to Saturday service at my own church and found out that the food bank was open for the day. I was able to get some vegetables and apples, potatoes, yams, collard greens, and onions. When I left, I went back to my sister's church for the food bank and got canned goods, pastas, and three packs of meat. I was telling God beforehand how I needed to choose between paying my gas bill or eating. And look what God did; he fed me for the entire week! Praise God!

My niece called and wanted to spend time with her mom as well as drop her son off to spend some time with his grandma. We were on our way to the grocery store, and my niece wanted to get picked up from the rapid station. I told my sister that I wanted to put my groceries away first, and my niece got mad and said that she would walk.

"Well, okay," I said.

As we were driving down the street, my niece and nephew were walking up the street on the opposite side toward us.

I said, "They got here fast." As we were pulling up on them, my sister told my niece that we were going to turn around so that they could get in the car. We turned around and pulled up beside them, and my niece kept walking as if she didn't see us. I saw the look on her face at first glance. I thought she was tired. But as they got into the car, I said, "Hey y'all, hey man," to my nephew, and my niece didn't say anything. She grumbled and looked upset, more like angry.

I asked, "What's wrong with you? Don't you hear me speaking to you? I haven't done anything to you." So she said something mean or grumbled. "You are in my car, what's up?" She said, "I didn't ask you to pick me up."

I was a bit shocked at the unknown attitude toward me, so I said, "Well, you can get out." I felt that evil spirit. I knew what that was. I felt my legs getting that nervous weak feeling, so I knew. I began to pray and rebuke that spirit off of each of us and out of my car. I told her that she could get out and take that evil spirit with her. She said, "I can, me and my baby."

My sister asked me not to put her out as I pulled to the curb. She said we were almost there. I got to my mom's house and remained in the car as they got out. My mom was on the porch talking with her neighbor, so l waited until they finished, then I warned my mom of my niece's attitude. My mom went in the house to tell my niece that she didn't want any drama, and my niece went on and on about something she heard that I said about her. I knew nothing about what she was talking about. After about an hour and a half, I left. She had caused a big scene, and I didn't want any part of it. Later on, my niece called from an unknown number and tried to apologize, but I didn't want to hear it. I'm still working on this area of forgiveness. Some actions just cut deeper than others for me.

God Will Make a Way

July 30, 2018

Today went well, yet I felt a bit worried about my finances. I knew that I was not to worry about my life, for God knows my needs, but God also says in Philippians 4:6 (KJV), "Be careful for nothing; but in everything by prayer and supplication with thanksgiving let your request be made known unto God." So I prayed, and I asked. I prayed for strength to not worry and just trust in God. Then I asked for financial help because my bills were due. Work had been cut down, so I was left with the decision to pay bills or be late with my rent. Or will my check even be enough to make my rent payment? Will my gas get cut off? I asked the Lord to bless my lottery ticket. So I was just a little weary, and I didn't like feeling this way.

I felt as if I could cry at any moment, then I felt as if I just wanted to leave this earth and be with the Lord. Then I felt as if I just wanted to do the Lord's will. Then I felt as if I was just patiently waiting. God does everything in his own time. I'd been listening to these videos by a woman named Sister Clare on YouTube. She has talks with Jesus; her channel is "Love Letters from Jesus." She talked about how Jesus said, "Let go of the way you want to hear me and accept my way." My spiritual sister from work introduced me to this site. They really helped me understand a lot. She speaks on politics as well. Her voice is very soft and calming. At first I didn't think I could listen to her, but after a few minutes, I got used to her voice, and I had listened to eight of her videos so far, six in one day. She has some very interesting topics.

I was trying to stay positive. I'd learned that God will leave you, or shall I say he will be silent just to test your faith. The devil and spirits were on the attack of my spirit, but so far, I had passed the test. My faith in Jesus and the Lord our Father is strong, and I didn't feel as if I could stray away no matter how I felt. I trust in the Lord always. The devil doesn't stand a chance. I would get to my destiny that God has for me, and I would learn who I was in Christ. The devil had enough of my time distracting me, so he can kick rocks. I was yearning and running for Jesus and God's heart. *Amen!*

August 3, 2018

Yesterday I received a phone call from the elder at the church. I had left him a voice message two days ago. He seemed surprised that his wife hadn't reached out to me as of yet. So he gave me his email address and asked me to write about all that I was going through, and he would forward the email to his wife. I agreed.

Later on, his wife gave me a call. I was at work at the time, but I talked anyhow. I was so ecstatic to hear from her. We discussed briefly all the events that were going on in my life. She gave me a few pointers about dreams and journaling and protecting your gift. She said that it sounded as if I had a good grasp on my dreams. She asked me how I knew about her. I said God sent me. After about thirty minutes, she asked me to pray about whether she was the one, and she would pray about it as well. I told her I would.

After I got home, I prayed and asked God if she was the one, and immediately, he said yes. I said, "That was fast." Let me ask again because I wasn't sure if it was me answering myself or not, and I received another yes. So I said, "Lord, I hope you don't get tired of me asking you questions over and over, but I need to ask you again to be sure for myself, but I'll wait until the morning." I knew God laughed at me, for I laugh at myself sometimes.

This morning when I woke up, I asked God if she was the one. I couldn't remember her name, so God said her name for me, but I was still trying to think of her name. I said "sister, I mean elder," and God said she's the one. Then I stopped and said, "Oh, I caught it, God. I heard you. She's the one. Okay, thank you."

I decided to wait until later on in the day to email her back. I wanted to ponder the thought a little longer. So at about 5:00 p.m., I emailed her and gave her my answer. Now I was awaiting her response. I prayed that God was putting us together, but if not, God would surely get me together himself. So I was patiently waiting and staying faithful.

Today, Carlos got discharged from Regency Hospital, and he was now back at the Normandy. Praise God in the highest!

Joy

August 6, 2018

Today was a good day. Work was calm, and I came home to take a nap. The clouds looked—well, I mean to me, they had no uniform as they usually did. They looked messy. I soon found out why they were looking like that. There was a thunderstorm that lasted about thirty minutes. It was rough, and it blew out the transmitter in my neighborhood just as I was about to put a plate of food in the microwave to warm it up. I called off work because I didn't want to come home to darkness, and I didn't want to leave Maxie here like this. So it was a great night to write and talk to God.

During my nap, I had a brief dream about Carlos. He called me on the phone, and he sounded so happy when I caught his voice. I asked him how could he be calling me and talking. He said, "I just started talking." I got so excited as I was screaming with joy that I felt my heart race as I lay asleep. I remembered someone being with me. I thought it was Ciauna and his dad, but that's a little blurry. The next thing I knew, before I could tell anyone, I woke up. I guess that's why God was taking his time with me. He knew I'd give myself a heart attack, haha.

I received an email back from my spiritual sister and elder yesterday. My spiritual sister was happy for me and was sending me a gift. The elder said,

Praise God for him answering you!

I also received a fairly quick answer.

I will reach out to you later this week. I'm still praying. I don't take helping someone with their "walk" lightly! I want to be sure that I have been assigned to help you. In the meantime, please feel free to contact me if you need spiritual guidance. My apologies for not responding back sooner than now. (Please don't give out my number.).

So I thanked her. Holy Spirit had told me to check my email, although I had been checking it all day. I also went to church service, and it was great. I was a little sleepy after work, but I maintained. I sat next to a guy that looked familiar to me. I later realized that we used to work together at The Crowne Plaza years ago. Pastor announced that he had lost his wife this past week. After he said his name, I knew for certain who he was. I told him who I was, and he couldn't hear me because of all the talking in the background, then someone else called him and took his attention away. I recalled hearing about some guys jumping him and robbing him and how he had suffered severe injuries. He had also gained some weight, so he looked a little different.

Pastor appeared to lock eyes on me two times during service. This was the third service that he had done this. I felt as if he saw or sensed something godly about me. This happened while I was in different sections of service. He seemed thrown off of his message afterward. He began to talk about how members should join some of the committees or volunteer at the campuses or even hug him so that our faces could become familiar to him.

I asked God if I was right about how I was feeling, and he said yes. I mean I could just tell that he sensed something special about me. I was going to start going to Bible study at the main campus on Wednesdays. Maybe I would meet the elder or at least see her. My spirit was getting very strong. I could feel and sense things so much more now, and my excitement for growth is eagerly awaiting more connection.

August 7, 2018

Well, my Los Man is still here with us fighting, and God was giving him strength. Since I last wrote, Carlos had fought two infections and won. He had fought pneumonia and was put on a ventilator, but he overcame that. He was looking a little worn, but now he was back to looking like himself again. Praise God the Most High.

I continued to feed him the gospel every time I visit. He was in a new room again, 811, since he returned from Regency Hospital a few days ago. He had a roommate now. I praise God for Carlos's strength and will to live. He could move more now. He would lift his hips to readjust himself. He belched three times in a row on one occasion, and his dad and I were ecstatic. He could follow more demands—squeeze your hand, give you his hand, and move his toes. His eyes still have trouble focusing.

I could tell that he was ready to wake up. I told him to hang in there; it wouldn't be much longer. He would start to really move when he heard my voice or his dad's. Physical therapy started putting hand and arm braces on him today. It helped his muscles to relax in his arm. Praise God, the staff seemed caring in this hall.

August 9, 2018

I watched the installation of Pastor John Gray to Relentless Church. It aired on June 3, 2018. I just came across it today. It was so wonderful.

I asked God if this was something like what I would experience when I was ready to minister to people, and he said yes. What a wonderful feeling I felt, and I just smiled at the moment to come. Pastor John Gray said he cried for two days for the joy of this day. I knew exactly how he felt. God has a way of making you feel so joyful when you never knew that you could feel more joyous.

God Is Silent

August 11, 2018

These last couple of days, I had been feeling a little lonely. I hadn't really heard God's voice, nor have I heard from the elder. I was not sure why. I knew that God moves in his own time, so I had no choice but to be patient. I was so glad that I'd been introduced to Clare's YouTube channel, because she has interesting and relevant topics that pertain to my life. I knew that Holy Spirit led me to her during my waiting period, I learned a lot from Clare. As I waited on the elder's response, Holy Spirit did a great job at leading me to scripture, podcast, and words of encouragement and verses of learning. So my learning and my gaining of wisdom and knowledge didn't cease. I just longed to hear Jesus, Holy Spirit, or the Lord. I developed a fatal attraction for them. I invited them into my dreams before I go to sleep at night or anytime.

Lately, my heart had grown more sensitive and passionate towards others. I felt for the mishaps of others, their illnesses and troubles. When I prayed for others, I felt my heart ache, and I would cry as I prayed for them. I was really beginning to feel bad for those that didn't know the Lord. I was looking forward to the day when the world would come together and call upon the Lord and rejoice as one. At times I wished that I could just be with the Lord, but I knew that I had a job to do first. To be able to give someone hope made my soul smile. Jesus's gift is so amazing. To know that he would use me as a vessel to touch others was beyond the joy that I could express in words. Until then, I would continue to praise, worship, and learn God's Word.

Seeking a Way to Serve

August 17, 2018

Well, today I felt much better. My head started hurting in the afternoon of August 13. I got dressed for my evening job, and my head started hurting really bad. I took some pain pills and a nap, but it didn't work, so I called off from work. I prayed that the pain would stop. I tried healing myself, but the pain got worse. I got nauseated, weak, and my head felt as if someone was pushing a needle through the back of my eye. I kept praying the healing prayer, "Pain, stop in the name of Jesus," over and over until I fell asleep. The medicine wasn't working. The next day was even worse. I could only get up to take Maxie out to relieve herself and then back to bed. I finally got up to brush my teeth and fix myself some grits and hot tea. I didn't eat it all.

I went back to bed and slept the entire day except for letting Maxie out once more. I made myself a cup of hot water and honey but fell asleep before finishing the entire cup. The next day, Thursday, I felt a little better. I continued to pray and listen to the Word. I tried healing myself over and over, never doubting God's power for he said that there are times when he won't allow the healing, for his will is his will. So I stood as strong as I could and remained faithful through it all. I wasn't going to let the devil win. Later that afternoon, I felt good enough to fix myself some sausage, eggs, grits, and hot tea. My head was still aching but not nearly as bad. I slept until time for my evening job at 5:30 p.m.

I made it to work, but I was still feeling weak and tired. My headache eased with the medicine that I took, and with lots of prayer, I made it through my shift. Praise God. Holy Spirit put it in my mind to email the elder since I hadn't heard from her. At times I was still not sure of the voice because I had been thinking and watching for her response. So I was patiently waiting on God and Holy Spirit.

After church service on Sunday, I signed up for the children's ministry and the catering and hospitality ministry. I got word back from both of them on Thursday. I emailed the elder, and she responded and asked if we could meet and talk. I said sure. It was nice of her to respond and ask to meet with me.

Well, at least work went well today and my visit to Carlos. He had some bloody mucus coming up when he coughed. The nurse checked his lungs and said she heard some rattling, so she ordered a chest x-ray. Another nurse suctioned his throat and gave him a breathing treatment. He looked okay to me, just a little coughing. He had this one aide who seemed to care about him a lot. That's great. I had to get her name.

August 18, 2018

After visiting Carlos yesterday, the thought of something being wrong with him hit me like a ton of bricks. On my way home, my heart began to ache for him, and the thought of why I kept having these migraines came over me. God wasn't answering me of why I was having the migraines. I prayed my health was fine. This rash on my back wouldn't go away, and now Carlos was getting a chest x-ray.

I started crying and asked God to forgive me if he thought that I was doubting his promise to heal Carlos. I prayed for forgiveness of my pain for him. I didn't know if it was okay to cry over Carlos because God gave me his promise. So I just asked for God to please understand that I was trying really hard to be strong, and sometimes it was just hard. I prayed, *Lord, please don't get upset with me for my sadness.* Later that evening as I drove to work, and I was admiring the formation of the clouds, there in the midst of the formation was a cloud shaped like a heart. It was darker than the rest of the clouds, so it was noticeable to me.

I knew it was God telling me that he loved me. It warmed my heart as I smiled. I took a picture of it and shared it with my family. God sure knew when to pick me up and reassure me. God is an awesome God. How could I ever leave him? After a few hours at work, my head began to ache again, this time on the left side near my temple. I took some meds, prayed for strength to get through my shift, and drank some water. As soon as I got home, I went to bed and prayed for the Lord to take the pain away in Jesus's name. I wondered if I was having these headaches for the suffering of someone else, or did I need to pray on someone's behalf. I was bewildered about why I was having migraines. It had been years since I'd had one this severe and for this many days.

This morning I woke up feeling a bit better. My headache was much calmer and bearable. When I got to work, I talked to my spiritual work sister. She was glad to see that I had signed up for the women's Bare It All Conference. I told her about my headaches. She said sometimes it was the spirit of infirmities that we had to pray off. She also said that it was okay to cry over Carlos because I am a mom and he is my baby and God knows my heart. That made me feel better. I'd grown up with the mentality that once you give it over to God, you are not to worry about it. But I guess he still knows that I am human, and maybe I was misunderstanding what God means about worrying about things. Some situations are different when it comes to your feelings. Carlos is my son, and God understands a mother's heart goes out to her children, even if she knows her child belongs to God.

The talk with my spiritual work sister helped, and I felt better. I told her about my dream as another coworker listened in. They thought that it was very interesting. I made it through my shift, but my headache began to come back, mildly. I went to the Word Church to serve the children's ministry. Everyone was very kind. I was working beside three ladies and one male. The teens were all so very pleasant and well-mannered.

Toward the last hour, my migraine began to get strong. I felt the weakness and nausea coming on. My meds did nothing. After we served, I ate one of the turkey hoagies, but I could only get half down because of the nauseating feeling. We also served tacos; the smell of the meat wasn't helping at all. I joked earlier at work that I was pregnant by Holy Spirit because those were the symptoms I was having. I went straight home and went to bed. I did manage to eat the other half of the sandwich on my way home. I knew that I needed to feed those meds and my head.

I woke up around 9:00 p.m. feeling better, so I walked Maxie for the night, and now I would fix myself a cup of hot tea and try another half of a sandwich. I didn't want to overdo my eyes by writing too much, but I would get a scripture in as well. I was supposed to visit Carlos, but I'd explain to him why I couldn't come tomorrow when I see him. So let me put this pen down before Ms. Migraine returned.

One Year Anniversary

August 28, 2018

Today make one year since Carlos's accident, and the Lord was still doing a great work in him. Thank God. This week had been very trying. I received a study Bible from my spiritual sister and her husband. It's pink and brown, leatherlike material and beautiful.

I was worried about Carlos's breathing on my last visit, and a chest x-ray was ordered. It came back negative. His dad visited him the next day and spoke to a nurse about his breathing, and another chest x-ray was ordered, and some mucus and fluid buildup was found, so he was given meds to help clear it up, yet his breathing remained the same. The nurses were suctioning him regularly, but it was doing him no good. On Thursday, Carlos had to be rushed to emergency. When he got there, he could barely breathe. Six doctors had to work on him, and he was very close to having to be resuscitated twice. They discovered that his airway was blocked by mucus and a blood clot. But once they got it unclogged, his breathing got better. One of the nurses told me that I should report the Normandy for neglect. I didn't have the strength for that right now. I'd pray about it. He was at Fairview Hospital, in ICU. Today he's getting a CAT scan on his belly because he hadn't had a bowel movement since he'd been there. They were checking for any

144

obstruction. When I came in to visit him, I was a bit thrown off because he had two extra tubes hooked up to him.

Over the weekend, I went to the Bare It All Women's Conference. My daughter and sister joined me on Friday. The experience was great. I did a lot of praying, worshipping, praising, and crying. Holy Spirit said it was time for me to allow others to pray for me and help me carry this load. So I did, and I cried for the entire two-day event. It was much needed and nice to have the ladies pray over me and to feel Holy Spirit along with God's presence each day.

After Carlos's episode, I asked the Lord for some reassurance on his recovery, and I received a dream Thursday night. I was over at a former coworker's house with another coworker and a few others from Carnegie Care Center where we all used to work together. I asked my coworker where Menorah Park Nursing Home was at, and she said across the field. It was a dirt field with large construction trucks passing through it. I was ducking and dodging the trucks trying to get across the field. I couldn't see the home, so I asked again and was told that "it was right there, you can't miss it."

A white van pulled up, and Carlos was on it. He was moving from seat to seat, not really able to sit up straight on his own. He was fidgety. A male nurse aide buckled himself and Carlos in the front passenger seat together. I smiled and said, "Be careful with him. He's a handful." I shut the van door, and they pulled off.

God said the devil is a lie. Carlos belongs to me, and I was still working on him. The Lord saved him once again. I was so grateful. The women at the conference kept asking me to let it go. But they didn't know that I was just overwhelmed with God's greatness and how he saved my Los Man once again. So I wasn't crying tears of sadness; they were tears of thanks as I battled the devil trying to keep me upset with the Normandy about the incident.

I was extremely upset, but I had prayed about it, and I had calmed down. The Lord said he had Carlos and wouldn't let anyone harm him, so I stood firm in that word, for God isn't ready to call him home just yet. Oh, I told the Normandy that if God wanted to take Carlos, I could deal with that because that's his will but not a man taking him due to neglect; no I couldn't handle that. Well, Carlos just returned from the CT scan. I prayed all was well. His breathing was a little heavy, so they would suction him shortly. He had a tube down his nose to drain his abdomen. Poor fella couldn't get a break. But his breakthrough was coming sooner than later. I believed, in Jesus's name.

Scattered Emotions

September 7, 2018

My Los Man is still here by the grace of God. This month had been filled with trials, setbacks, and triumphs. He spent two weeks at Fairview Hospital and was currently on week one at Regency Hospital. God continued to work great works in Carlos. He had beaten four infections and pneumonia. He was due to go back to the Normandy, but the doctor decided against it because he wasn't passing his stool and had an infection, and his eyes still wasn't cleared up from the infection. He started out in a room by himself, then after a couple of weeks, he was moved to a room with a roommate. He was elderly and had visitors regularly. They were kind and understanding toward us and our prayers and worship. Carlos was off of the ventilator and had two more antibiotics to finish before being discharged. He was looking better but didn't seem to focus on me or anything.

I had a dream the other day. Just when I was thinking about how I hadn't dreamt of my Los Man, God gave me a dream. Praise God! I couldn't help but to love God. In the dream I had, I went over to Carlos's dad's house, and when I opened the door, Maxie was there. She was walking around as Carlos and his dad sat next to each other. She was sniffing the floor as if getting familiar with her surroundings.

I asked with bewilderment how Maxie got to their house. His dad said that one of my coworkers from the embassy had brought her over. I asked why. And he said because Maxie wouldn't stop barking, and the neighbors were complaining, so she went to my house and got her. Carlos was speaking to me. I believe he was saying that Maxie was barking a lot as well. All the time while I was speaking to his dad, his dad was tapping me or nudging me on my leg saying, "Look, he is talking to you." I looked down, and with much excitement I yelled, "Carlos!" I started kissing him all over his face. During the entire conversation the idea or thought that Carlos was sitting up in a chair, fully aware, never dawned on me, until his dad made me notice.

God was always giving me hope which strengthened me constantly.

I also had a dream that my ex and I had gotten back together, or somehow we were in the same house, and he wouldn't let me leave. I was yelling to him that I wanted to go home, and I was kicking my legs. I was on the bed, I believe. He grabbed my face and told me if I didn't stop, he was going to yell at me. And he said, "Now give me a kiss so that I can go." He took the kiss.

I got up to look around the house to see if I could escape. I went into a bathroom, and there were two toilets. That was odd to me. I walked through another room. It was dark because the lights were out. It was decorated with wooden walls and fixtures. It was actually furnished well and kept up nicely. I proceeded to go into another room and heard voices. The house was divided as if it was a side-by-side duplex, but there was no wall, nor door to separate the rooms. I looked across the room to the other side, and there was a hallway where two people were talking to a man with an animal. It looked like a tiger, and the man had a tiger face as well. I believe they were two ladies. As I peeked in on the conversation, I got the courage to just leave the house. As I was looking at them, the tiger turned into a kitten, and the man transformed as well. They turned and noticed me, but I got out, and the dream was over.

So I looked up dreams of tigers: the tiger is a symbol of ferocity and fearsomeness. It is also a spirit animal that represents the feeling of raw emotions and power. It can represent uncertainty. So when I woke up, I remember saying to God, "I know this doesn't mean that I'm getting back with my ex, because, God, you know that I don't want to go backward." This explanation of the dream told me why I got the courage to leave the house. I am fearless.

Today as I was napping, I dreamt that I walked in on a worship service at work, and the speaker directed someone over to pray for me, and as they did, the person was a coworker at the embassy. My spiritual sister was there also. As I leaned on the counter to pray, there were multiple used super packets on the counter, pink, blue, and white. I was picking them up, and as I felt Holy Spirit come over me, I began to cry hard, and my coworker was holding my shoulders and hugging me from behind. I remember calling Jesus's name over and over as I cried and worshipped. Then I was awakened from my nap. I could feel Holy Spirit, and I let him know that I felt his presence. I love my Lord so much; I could never imagine ever being without him. Thank you, Jesus, for abiding in me.

Today I went to my first grief recovery class. It was orientation. There were fourteen women and one instructor. He said that we all must talk or leave the class. The women all had their own issues of grief, and I believed this course would be beneficial. The instructor asked why we were here. My first thought was to say for ministry or to serve on one of the ministries. But as I listened to some of the women, Holy Spirit told me that I was there to let out some of my emotions that I was dealing with concerning Carlos and my family. So that's what I told the group as I cried while I spoke. I felt myself not really wanting to talk, but I got it out anyway. The Lord knew I needed an outlet for some of this pain. I knew it was for my good and the good of my journey. I was looking forward to completing this course.

I was here visiting Carlos. He looked swollen in the face and neck. He sounded full of phlegm, but the nurse says that his vitals and all were good. I spoke to the head nurse, and he would order a chest x-ray to be safe.

I read a few chapters on healing to Carlos as I held his hand. He held my hand tightly and kept lifting up as he strained to cough, and he squeezed my hand even tighter. I couldn't tell if he was in pain or discomfort, so I prayed for his relief. His eyes were red as well. He turned very red when he coughed and sounded so congested. I prayed that he wasn't in pain and truly heard my prayers and the gospel music I played for him. I prayed it gave him strength as much as it gave me.

Testing of My Faith

A new doctor came in Carlos's room. He looked Indian, medium build, and handsome. But when he spoke to me, it was with no compassion. He asked me if I was family, and I said that I'm his mom. He looked confused and asked me what my relationship to Carlos was again; I said his mother. He spoke very softly though. He said that he had heard a little about what happened to Carlos, so I told him that he was in a car accident in August of 2017 and was thrown from the car, injuring his brain on the left, right, and back with damage to his brain stem. He stared at me with a look of sadness.

When I said brain stem, he sat down next to me saying that he wanted to hear me better. He asked me if I came to see Carlos every day. I said, "Just about. If I'm not here, his dad is." He said it must be tough for him and his quality of life. I looked at him puzzled and said, "Well, he is much better than when he started." He said, "Well, but his quality of life…" I said, "God has him. He will be okay." He asked, "Does he do anything." I said, "He can open his eyes. He can hear. He knows when I'm in the room because he starts moving when he hears me." He went on to say, "But his quality of life, it must be hard for you." I said, "Well, I have hope in God and faith that he will get better." He said, "Hope is

151

always good." And I said, "Not only hope but faith in Jesus that he will pull him through."

He stood and walked over to Carlos to check him and asked if he would open his eyes. I said, "Yes, and he will squeeze your hand." So I started to tell him that Carlos had just gone to sleep and might not respond. He was in and out. I called his name, and he cracked his eyes open. The doctor looked at me and said, "He opened them only a little." I said, "He can open them all the way. He's just tired. He has been awake since I've been here." I tickled his foot, and he pulls back. "He is ticklish." The doctor smiled at that motion and left the room.

I prayed over Carlos, and my heart was heavy as I held back my tears. The doubt that was on the doctor's face and the sound of his voice was so painful for me. I hurried out of the hospital, and as soon as I got outside, the tears fell. I got to my car and just cried and prayed and stayed on God's promise. My entire ride home, I was crying and praying. When I got home, Maxie was happy to see me, but I couldn't speak to her. I went straight to my prayer room and fell on my knees and prayed that Jesus would come and show the doctors and nurses his miracle hands at work on Carlos. I prayed so, so hard.

Holy Spirit reminded me of all the dreams of Carlos recovering and how it was Satan using one of his evil spirits to work through the doctor to cause me doubt. After a short nap, I recovered and thanked Holy Spirit for reminding me that God has the last say, not man, nor science, and certainly not Satan. I went about my evening with confidence in Jesus and Holy Spirit that abides within me.

September 13, 2018

Today Carlos looked much better. He wasn't as swollen, and his breathing sounded better, not much coughing, but there was still blood in his mucus. I talked to him and reassured him that it was not man that we were depending on, but it was God's word that we were standing on, God's promise alone. We would remain faithful to God no matter what the doctor said. I told Carlos to pray and asked God to forgive him for all his sins and to listen to God and the angels.

I told two nurses of my experience with the doctor yesterday, and they did not think that was acceptable. Carlos had slept most of the visit today. I hoped it was only due to him being tired and not an illness. I read six chapters on healing from the Bible and played the seventh chapter in audio from my phone. We listened to some gospel music as well. I would go home to pray for the doctor again. This time I would call out his name, I believed it would be more effective. My pastor said to say the name when you pray for someone.

September 20, 2018

I had been feeling a little distant, as if Jesus had been busy with other tasks and had me on hold. I prayed for the doubt and unbelief to be removed for I knew it was just an evil spirit that wanted me to feel alone. I was also struggling with going out and trusting Jesus wholeheartedly. It was hard when I couldn't see how I was going to pay my bills. I was in-between jobs, and the one I was just starting (Paws Play) was slow right now, but it was picking up. I constantly told myself to trust Jesus for he wouldn't let me down, nor have me quit one job or both without having a way for me to be financially able to sustain during the process.

I had a dream of Carlos. He was much younger than he is now. He was a teenager, around sixteen, and was sitting on the porch with a young lady who was just about the same age. I had never met her. They were laughing and enjoying themselves. His dad was there, and I asked him if he thought that Carlos remembered anything, and he said that Carlos told him that he did. So I asked Carlos if he remembered the accident, and he said yes but showed no signs of sadness. I asked him again, and he said yes. I was hoping that he didn't. I didn't know why, but I didn't want him to remember.

Carlos was playing with a baby who looked to be maybe 5–6 months old. He was holding the baby up over his head. I asked Carlos what happened, and he said that he was driving and playing with the baby, and they crashed. I didn't understand. The girl sitting on the porch with him was playing with the child as well. It seemed as if they were in their own world.

I had forgotten about this dream, so I asked Holy Spirit to recall it back to me, and he did. So now I asked for clarification of the dream. I believe I had another dream this night as well. So I asked for recollection of it.

I'd been feeling as if when Carlos woke up, I wanted to have a family celebration but only with those that showed true concern and support. I felt as if that was selfish, but at the same time, I didn't feel selfish. I was going to have Jesus lead me in this decision.

Today my Los Man was moved from ICU to a regular room. Praise God! He also looked better. He had been awake for most of the visit. I thanked God for his progress always. We shall stand on God's promise and keep moving forward.

Facing Reality

October 15, 2018

Well, a lot had happened since I last wrote in this journal. Carlos's kidneys failed, and we had to decide if we wanted him to be put on dialysis. I was at work the morning that the doctor told me this, so on my lunch break, Holy Spirit led me to the huge Catholic Church here downtown. I asked Holy Spirit if it was okay for me to go there, and he said they believe in Jesus as well, so I went in and asked the security guard if it was okay for me to come in and pray. He said yes. Oh, my heart was so heavy and full of pain; I could barely speak. I proceeded to the back as my eyes welled up with tears, and my heart ached so. I had been praying to my Lord and asking him to help Carlos and make his pain and sickness go away. But I felt the need to be surrounded by the spirit. I was glad to be in the church.

I prayed and worshipped with the 15–20 people that were already there at the church. The feeling and presence of the Lord was so strong and apparent. I worshipped for I believe about thirty minutes or so, and I cried myself until my head ached. After I left, I felt so much better. I could feel that the Lord heard me and lifted some of the pain from me. I thanked the Lord, stopped and got some lunch, and went back to work.

When it came time to make the decision for Carlos to be put on dialysis, the kidney nurse said that he would have to go immediately. There was a staff nurse in the room taking care of Carlos, and I asked her opinion. She was hesitant. She said that it could prolong his life. I asked if she thought that it was necessary or would it help him. She looked at me with concern and asked me if anyone had explained what was going on with Carlos, the stages of what was happening? I said no. She said, "Not even his doctor?" I said, "No, why, what's going on?"

We stepped out into the hallway, and another lady doctor came. I asked them to please tell me everything. If it was not going to help him, I wouldn't do it. They were still hesitant. I said, "Really, I'm good. I can handle it. I have God, and he has told me anyway." The one doctor said, "So you are spiritual. Good, okay then. This is something that's beyond me, but we believe that his body is shutting down naturally." She began to express her sympathy and to tell me how her dad went through something similar, and she had to make a decision. She said the good thing about Carlos's situation was that the decision to let him go had been made naturally, so that wouldn't be a burden on us.

I had previously told the kidney doctor to schedule his appointment to have a shunt put in Carlos. He was so swollen, eyes red, and he looked so miserable. I felt so bad for him. My heart just ached. The day before when I had gone to visit him, he was lying in bed, eyes wide open. Vomit was all over his neck and trachea. His clothes were wet with urine. I just cried. It hurt me so bad, and now as I wrote, the ache returned as well as the tears. He was having trouble breathing. I went to get a nurse and asked her if she could clean him up. She said he was next on her list and that he had just vomited. I didn't believe that of course.

After maybe 10–15 minutes, I sent for a nurse again. I had prayed over Los and apologized to him for the condition he was in. My sister was there with me. She left the room. I knew the sight of him like that hit her, and she didn't want me to know. The nurse came back, and they cleaned him up. She apologized and said that she would've been upset if she found her loved one like that as well.

So back to the discussion of dialysis. Carlos's appointment was made, but I had doubts. I felt Holy Spirit telling me not to do it. I thanked and hugged the two ladies for their honesty. I said that if it wasn't going to help him truly recover, that I wanted to let him go to be with the Lord. I asked them how I could make him comfortable and end his pain. They told me about hospice, but the lung doctor didn't think that he would last the ride home, but he would check his lungs and let me know the next day.

In the meantime, before this happened, I had three dreams or visions that I didn't want to share, nor come to terms with. Since they were negative to me, I thought it was Satan. I had thoughts of writing Carlos's obituary. I heard a voice say that he was going to succumb to his injuries. It was soft and gentle. I had a vision of faces coming from fire, many faces, but I didn't recognize them. They were only shapes. I had a dream of light above and darkness below; shapes of heads and hands were reaching out of the darkness. I asked the Lord if I was coming out of the darkness into the light. Then I dismissed it. I also had a vision of darkness on both sides and a ray of light coming down from the sky and shining right in the middle of the darkness; shapes of heads and faces were coming from both sides of the dark areas. Bodies started flying out of the darkness, and I realized they were angels because they had no feet. It looked like they had on robes. They flew into the light. I said, "Lord, my dreams and visions have been a bit strange lately." I subconsciously knew that my Los Man would be leaving me soon, yet not wanting to admit it, so I rebuked Satan from my mind, body, and spirit.

The day of Carlos's appointment to receive the shunt, my daughter and I were at the gym working out, and I talked to her about everything. She agreed that there was no need to put her brother through any surgery. So I called to cancel the appointment and asked to have him be made comfortable instead. The nurse said that she would have to get the doctor to put in orders for it first.

The day before, when I walked into the room and had seen Carlos looking so distressed and miserable, all the visions of the darkness and light and spoken words came to me after I found out about his kidney failure. I lost it, for the reality that it was Holy Spirit telling me that Carlos was getting ready to be with the Lord hit me, and right then I knew, I truly knew he was leaving me. I prayed for strength and asked God, *If you are going to take him, please don't let him suffer. Make it fast. And if you are going to let him live, please heal him from the sickness and pain.* Oh, how my heart ached.

I spoke to Carlos's dad and explained what the nurses had told me, and he agreed to just let him go. He also told me that he had been told that Carlos's liver was going bad as well. So I knew that we were making the right decision.

On October 2, 2018, we called our family and told them of our decision to take Carlos off of the ventilator and allow him to go home to be with God. We agreed to let him transition at the hospital. The ride home was forty minutes, so we figured it wouldn't be long; he would be gone by nightfall. We had a lot of family support who came to say their goodbyes.

The nurse came in to explain the procedure after a couple of hours. She would give him some morphine and another medicine every couple of hours after they take him off of the ventilator. His brothers and one of his cousins couldn't bear to see him go, so they said their goodbyes and left.

Oh, before all this, some of my family were already at his bedside before I got there. I had told everyone to meet me at the hospital at noon. When I got there, I had seen the crowd and went to hug my eldest son, and I just broke. My knees buckled, and I got weak. He hugged me tightly and said, "I got you." I cried so hard as reality set in. My other son and daughter came over and held me as well. I held on to him for what seemed like hours. My son just held my hand as I stared at the wall. They were so strong for me.

I put on Pandora and played *Today's Gospel Hits*. We sang and worshipped all night long and listened to two sermons from Pastor John Gray. In the midst of our praise, I met my sister-in-law at the sink to wash my hands, and she said we should play music that Carlos liked and go out partying. I looked at her in such disagreement and said, "You've got to be kidding me. This is what he likes. He's going out with nothing but Jesus and goodness in his mind and on his heart. This is what he's been getting for thirteen months. No need for me to stop now."

We went back to his bedside and began singing. Holy Spirit sent her into a worship where she sang and praised the Lord as she cried. I was beside her singing as well, and I looked up and thanked the Lord for keeping me strong and not changing the station, nor mood, for I knew it was Satan trying to use her at that moment.

The ventilator was taken off of Carlos at around 5:15 p.m., and after about 3–4 hours, Carlos was still stable. He was breathing on his own, and his heartbeat was still strong. The nurse came in to check on him several times, and all she could do was shake her head and say how strong he was. It was getting late, and people were beginning to leave. They had to go to work, so around I guess close to 3:00 am, the last persons left. and it was myself, my aunt, daughter and his dad left to see him off to glory.

Oh, before my aunt left I said, "Well, Lord, it's been a couple of hours, and he is still here. You are more than welcome to do him like Lazarus and give us a miracle, for if you can wake Lazarus from the dead, then you can wake Carlos up too. Your will is your will, and I will go along with whatever you choose. Either give us a miracle or take him, but please relieve him from his suffering." I spoke those words more than once throughout the day and night.

My aunt said it was not time yet. I said, "That's because he's waiting on me to be ready." She said, "No, he isn't." Jokingly I said, "Yes, he is. God wants to make sure I'm ready." We went back and forth, laughing and smiling. I couldn't remember exactly what she was saying, but it was all in fun.

Oh, I believe she said to Carlos, "You ain't ready to go yet, are you, man?" But I knew God was preparing my heart. No matter how many times I told my son it was okay to go, God knew when it was time.

All night long, I sat by Carlos's bedside and rubbed his head, legs, arms. I kissed him and prayed over him as well as assured him that we would be okay. I soon dozed off while lying on his feet; music was still playing. I heard a man's voice very loud in my right ear say, "Carlos." It was deep and strong. I popped up, looked at Carlos. He was still asleep. I looked around the room.

Everyone was still in their places. They all looked at me with concern. His dad said, "What?" I shook my head and said, "Nothing." I was thinking, *Who said that? And did I hear that? No one heard that.* I put my head back down and turned the music off because I wanted see if I would hear the voice again.

I thought, *Well, maybe I should pray because his monitor had begun to beep more frequently.* So I picked up the phone to allow the Bible app to play. The book of Matthew came to mind first.

I said, "Well, Luke and John tell of Jesus as well." But Holy Spirit said Matthew first. I put the book of Matthew on audio and thought of how it introduces Jesus's genealogy, birth, and miracles before he died.

So I said, "Okay, Los. I'll introduce you to Jesus and let him hold your hand and walk you on up to heaven." So Matthew it was.

I got up and began folding the sheets and blankets that were left on the chairs and the ones I was using, for I felt the time getting near. As I walked over to stack the extra chairs, I looked back at Carlos, his eyes were open, and he was looking at me. I saw his head turn and fall to his left shoulder as he was opening his eyes. I felt weird and even said to myself, *Okay, Los, why are you looking at me like that?* I looked at his monitor, and it kept beeping. It was at 38 and 41 for heartbeat and breathing; I didn't recall which was for which.

My aunt said, "I see you looking at me, man," then added, "Donnie, he's looking at you."

I ignored her because I was still trying to process what was happening, and I knew he was.

She said again, "Donnie, he's looking at you. He says you about to make him late." I said, "He can't see me." She sat up closer and said, "Yes, he can. He said you better come on."

I looked back at him, and he was staring at me, his eyes following my every move. It was as if he was saying "Come on, Ma, I know you heard him call me." I felt everything he was thinking. By this time, my daughter had jumped up and said, "Yes, he is." His dad got up and came over to his bedside. I went to him and lifted up his head and tried to close his eyes so that he could just go, but they wouldn't close. I didn't know what I was thinking doing that. His dad whispered, "You are not supposed to close his eyes until he is gone." I just wanted him to go ahead and rest.

We gathered around him and began to pray as the book of Matthew played. We said our goodbyes and assured Carlos that it was okay to go home. I was about to turn the audio Bible off but didn't. As Carlos calmly took his last breath with no struggle, the last number I saw on the monitor was 38, then 0. He was gone in less than five minutes. A sense of peace filled the room. I looked around and said, "Do you feel that?" They said yes. We high-fived one another. I began walking around the room praising and thanking God. We said, "Well, all right then" as we high-fived each other again. My daughter held onto a chair and just worshipped and thanked the Lord as she cried out. I hugged his dad, then we had a group hug and continued to praise the Lord for he had lifted the pain from our hearts and souls. We felt so much peace and joy. It was the most amazing feeling to feel the gentle breeze come through the room. My God is *awesome*!

Hours before Carlos's death, my daughter had gone outside and came back overjoyed and excited, telling me to come outside, but I didn't want to leave Carlos's bedside. She said that the angels had opened up the gates of heaven, and God had moved a cloud from in front of the sun. The clouds were shaped like two angels on either side of the sun and the sky; it was beautiful. I smiled and told her that it was meant for her only. She was so ecstatic. She said, "I'm going back outside." And she left to admire the sky again. I looked out his room window. The sun was shining so bright, and it felt peaceful.

As Carlos's spirit ascended from his body, the sun rose. He left for his home in heaven at 7:17 a.m. as I ended the book of Matthew on chapter 17. I told them why I had jumped up from my sleep. I told them that I heard God call my baby for roll call. They were so amazed. They said they were wondering why I was looking around the room like that. My daughter said that she knew I would be the first to know when it was time.

The Lord put a stamp on Carlos's death by allowing our spirits to connect so that I could hear him call Carlos's name for roll call and assured me that he was going to heaven. One of my final requests concerning my Los Man was for the Lord to allow our spirits to connect one more time, and he did. Oh, how I love the Lord for he surely heard my cry!

My Los Man went to be with our Lord and Savior Jesus Christ on October 3, 2018, at 7:17 a.m. with Jesus in his heart, soul, and mind. I felt so joyful knowing that God is pleased with the way we sent him off and stood firm on our faith and trust in his word until the very last moment of Carlos's life. The book of Matthew ended on chapter 17 as Jesus was ascending to heaven, I believe.

On the ride home, we were still in awe of everything that happened, and I was still trying to understand how I heard God call Carlos and how my heart wasn't feeling any heaviness, nor ache. I was just feeling peaceful and wonderfully shocked.

All of a sudden, my daughter said "look, look" with excitement as she stared out the window, and when I looked to my left out of her back passenger window, flowing with the car was a huge pair of angel wings. It was so amazing that I turned my head back around, and she was still excited. I looked back again, and the wings slowly flew into the sky and got smaller and smaller until they were gone. They were so perfect and so real; I couldn't process the glory. It was such an amazing day.

I didn't have any life insurance on Carlos, and I didn't prepare plans for his death because I believed God would wake him up. And I didn't want God to think that I didn't trust him by planning Carlos's death. I wanted to trust God until the very end. His dad and I decided to cremate him, and my sister-in-law was so kind to give us the money to do it. There were people that wanted a viewing, and we didn't have the money. As I was standing in the kitchen talking to my daughter and her dad, Holy Spirit asked me if I wanted to have a viewing. I said, *Yes, well, I would like to have the whole thing.* And he said we'll have it. I looked at them and said we were going to have a funeral. They asked how. I said, "I don't know, but Holy Spirit asked me and I said yes and he said plan it." So we planned it.

I requested a minister from the Word Church to perform the services. Carlos attended the teen church services there and the adult services after his teenage years many times with his cousin as well as played basketball in the gym room there. Therefore, he was a frequent visitor even without me. That made me proud.

When I went to meet with the minister who would perform the services, as I sat down and the minister began to write, a dream came to me. I recalled that in the dream, I was planning his services, and the desk was a nicely polished brown wood with a tablet that had writing on it. I recalled asking myself why he wrote so sloppily when he could use the lines. The entire setup from the writing and positioning of the paper on the table was exact to the dream. This was a dream that I had rebuked, and all along God was preparing me for this moment. As I stared into space with awe, I said to my sister who was with me and the minister, "I have been here before. I've already done this." They both smiled at my excitement.

God touched my families' hearts near and far, and we were able to have a full funeral service for my Los Man. We had enough to pay our bills for the month and buy whatever extras that we needed to wear. The funeral home was packed, standing room only all the way out in the hallways. He was so loved. My sons, daughter, their dad, and I didn't shed a tear at the funeral. I worshipped as if I was at a church service. One of the pastors that was speaking at his service kept looking around the podium at me. I wondered if he was looking for a different reaction from me. After the service, I went to tell all the ministers thank you for their service, and he held my hand and said how there was a spirit of God on me. I said, "I know God is with me." He looked so amazed. I could feel Holy Spirit's presence as we spoke, and as I shook the hand of the lady minister that was present, her grasp was full of the spirit. I let them know that I felt his presence, and everything went perfectly. Thank you, Jesus, my Lord and Savior.

The Betrayal

After being so strong for the funeral, after a week, it was time to retrieve Carlos's ashes from the funeral home. Well, I thought I could do it by myself. I went to retrieve his ashes, and fear came over me. I got back to my car and realized that my child was really in this box, and I cried in that parking lot for maybe ten minutes. I called his dad and told him where I was. He said with such sympathy that he did not expect me to go alone.

Two weeks later, I sent his dad to get his belongings from the Normandy, and when he got there, he was told that they had gotten rid of all of Carlos's belongings. When asked why they didn't call us first, he was told that they got rid of the belongings thirty days after the departure. Well, it had only been two weeks. They said they start from the time he left the facility. When he told me that, my heart sank. So many thoughts went through my head. I didn't get to save anything from his accident, no scent on his blanket. I made his blanket and pillow, painted pictures, had a daily prayer book that I read to him on each and every visit. I was so upset; I thought of going viral on the Internet to tell what the Normandy had done. Then I wanted to sue. I just was numb as tears rolled down my eyes. They destroyed all my physical memories.

I called my mom and the Normandy to confirm. I felt as if they never expected him to return. I knew I felt the doubt from them, but as long as I kept my faith, it didn't matter. Yet seeing what they did hit hard. The ache in my heart was unbearable. I went into my prayer closet to pray and ask God what should I do. I was so very distraught. Before I could get one word out, Holy Spirit said I was to do nothing. I asked about the memories and all the items that I had handmade for him. Holy Spirit said, "You have all the memories you need. I will help you recall." I said, "But how could they do that? I didn't even get a phone call, nothing." I stayed in that closet on the floor with my head against the wall, crying for what seemed like hours, until I fell asleep before I agreed to what Holy Spirit said.

About maybe two weeks, I got a call from the social worker at the Normandy, and she said that they were cleaning out the storage room and came across some boxes that belonged to Carlos, and I was welcome to come get them. I was so ecstatic. I thanked her and God. When I got there, she wasn't in her office, so I left her a picture of a bird that I had painted in remembrance of Carlos, and I took my boxes. It contained his audio Bible, waterfall, pictures of his cousins and family, paintings that I had on the wall, and a few other items. No clothing or blankets that I could get a scent from, but I was grateful. And yes, God sent me a scent of Carlos and memories.

Reflection

During this season, I developed a real relationship with God. I learned that God talks to his children daily; we just have to stop and listen. Even though this was tough, I praised God even when it hurt and when I was lost for words. I learned what real love in Jesus feels like. I learned how to forgive others on a deeper level. I learned to examine myself when it comes to supporting others. I now understand that not everyone can, will, or even know how to show support; and it's okay. No love lost. I have learned to open up and talk of God's goodness and share my testimonies. I'm no longer uncomfortable about sharing God's Word. I took this time to allow God to change me from the inside out. God gave me signs, dreams, visions, and sent people to get me through this dark time in my life. God removed that ache in my heart and replaced it with peace that I can't explain and joy—unspeakable joy.

To the person who has lost a child or has ever had to endure the suffering and helplessness, I ask that you just hold on to God's Word, lean on him, and praise him through the pain. Pay attention to your dreams; look out for the signs. God will not let you go through the pain alone even when he is quiet. Hold on, and praise him for the moment, second, minute, hour, and day that you still have. Don't miss the miracles that he sends. He will reward you for your suffering. Above all else, pray without ceasing. I love you, but God loves you more.

A Champion Claiming Gods Victory

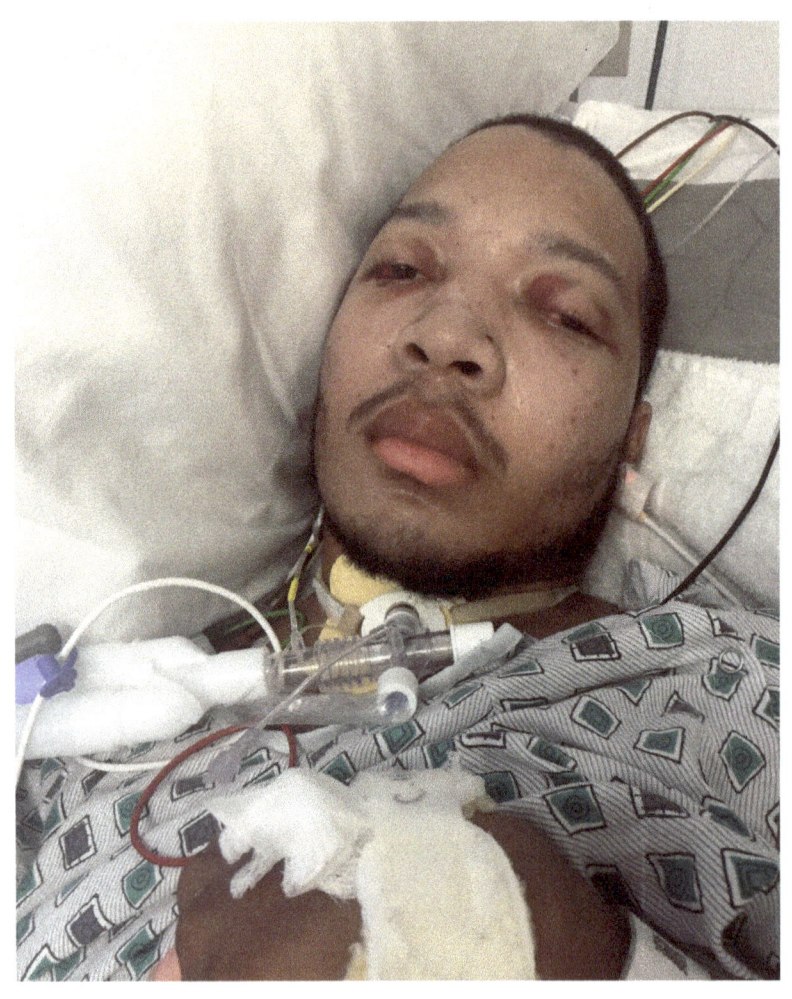

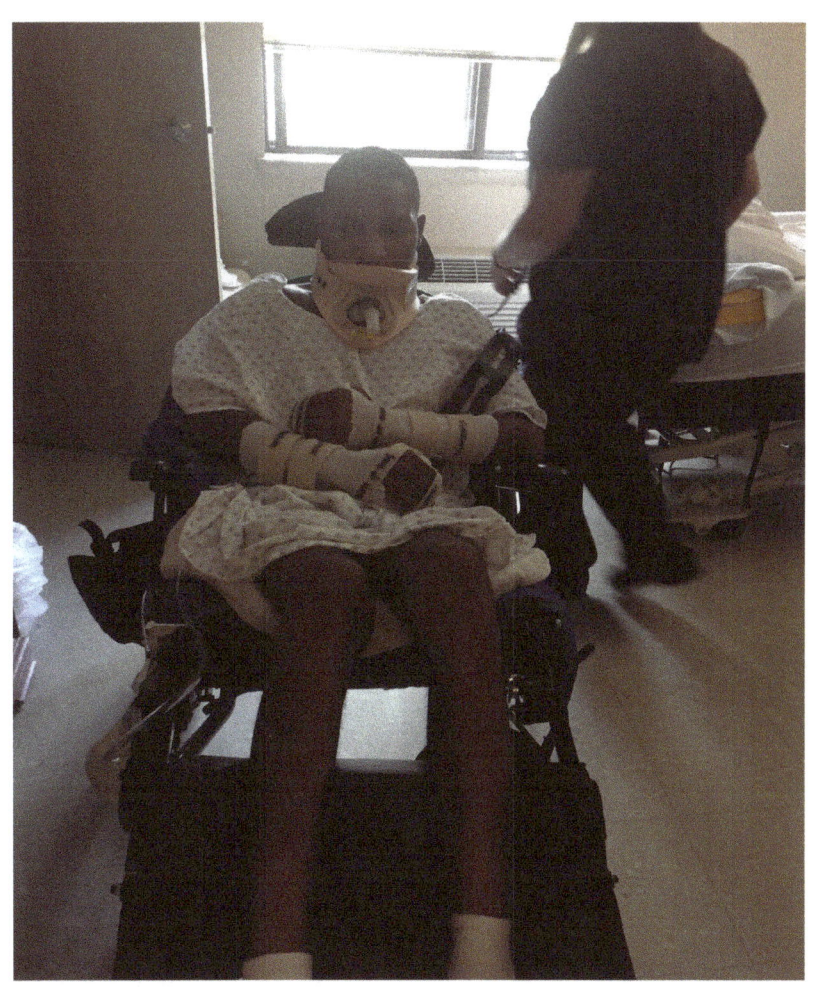

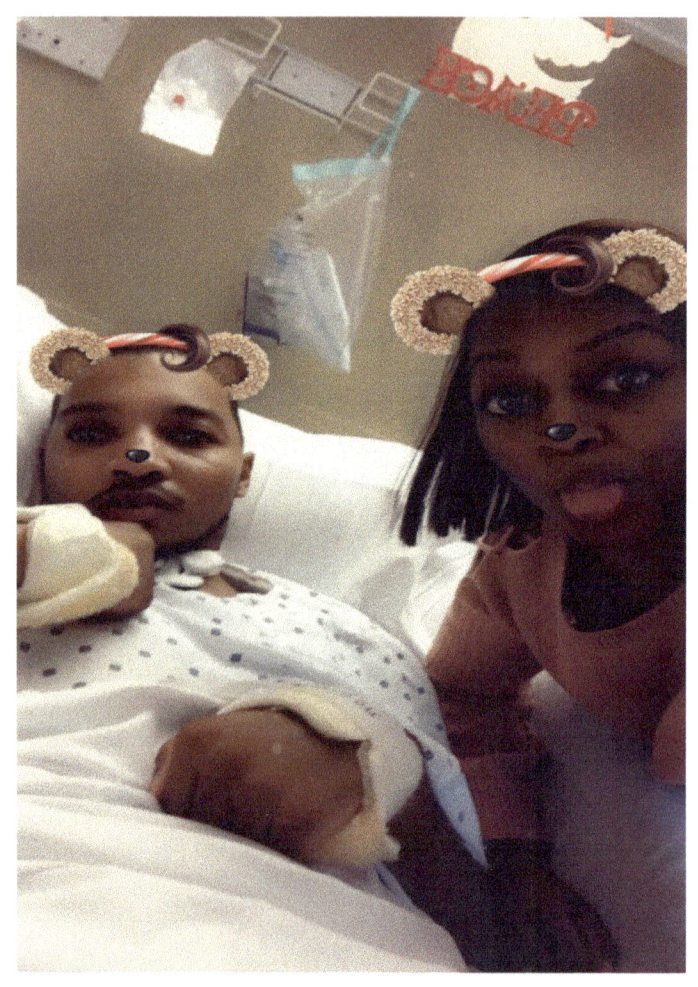

My dear son,
In times of pain, In times of grief, look to the skies and find relief. Draw your strength from the Heavens and let God lead your feet.

Hebrews 11:6
But without faith it is impossible to please him: for he that cometh to God must believe that he is, and that he is a rewarder of them that diligently seek him. Stay strong my son.

Love
Mom

Whenever
you feel down
look up to the sky.
Call out to your
"Guardian Angel"
and he will be right there
to lift you up again and again.

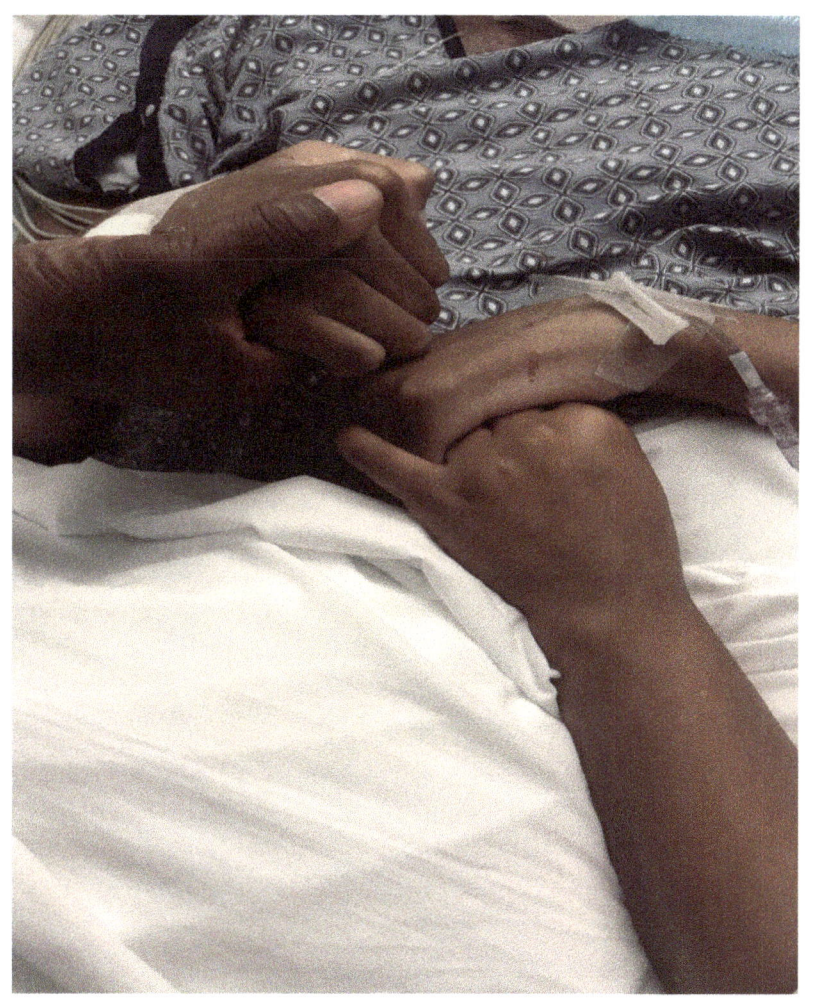

www.ingramcontent.com/pod-product-compliance
Lightning Source LLC
Chambersburg PA
CBHW051152120626
46547CB00012B/1057